BOOKS BY RICHARD MITCHELL

Less Than Words Can Say
The Graves of Academe
The Leaning Tower of Babel

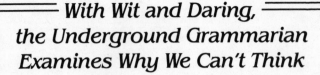
With Wit and Daring,
the Underground Grammarian
Examines Why We Can't Think

A Fireside Book
Published by Simon & Schuster, Inc.
New York

RICHARD MITCHELL

The
GIFT
of
FIRE

Copyright 1987 by Richard Mitchell
All rights reserved
including the right of reproduction
in whole or in part in any form
Simon and Schuster/Fireside Books
Published by Simon & Schuster, Inc.
Simon & Schuster Building
Rockefeller Center
1230 Avenue of the Americas
New York, New York 10020
SIMON and SCHUSTER and FIRESIDE and colophons are registered
trademarks of Simon & Schuster, Inc.
Designed by Karolina Harris
Manufactured in the United States of America

1   3   5   7   9   10   8   6   4   2
Library of Congress Cataloging in Publication Data
Mitchell, Richard.
The gift of fire.

"A Fireside book."
1. Philosophy.   2. Thought and thinking.   3. Education
—Philosophy.   I. Title.
B72.M55   1987   100   87-351
ISBN 0-671-64327-4
0-671-63938-2 (pbk.)

CONTENTS

INTRODUCTION

I SUSPECT THAT THOSE WHO have read some of my other works will be a little surprised by this one. I am a little surprised by this one.

That, in itself, is nothing new. I have never yet written anything, long or short, that did not surprise me. That is, for me at least, the greatest worth of writing, which is only incidentally a way of telling others what you think. Its first use is for the *making* of what you think, for the discovery of understanding, an act that happens only in language.

I have habitually found it convenient, and perhaps just a little too easy, to look for understanding by paying close attention to failures of understanding, which always take the form of bad language. Just as there is nothing but language in which to make sense, there is nothing but language in which to make nonsense. So, in my works, at least, the examination of sense and nonsense has ordinarily been a sometimes clever and amusing castigation of fools, who can be shown to imagine that they make sense when they don't.

The castigation of fools is, of course, an ancient and honorable task of writers and, unless very poorly done, an enterprise that will usually entertain those who behold it. No matter what else we imagine that we believe about the propriety of compassion for the unfortunate, we do like to see fools exposed. It's funny. And it is not only funny; it is the great theme of Comedy, and a mild, domestic counterpart of the great theme of Tragedy, in which we rejoice, however sadly, to see villains brought down.

So it is that the habitual contemplation of folly, which does not seem to be the worst thing in the world, leads little by little to some consideration of vice, which does seem to be the worst thing in the world. It is troubling to notice that when we are foolish or "only foolish," as we easily deem it, we find ourselves all the more likely to do bad things. And when we can see, as I think I have so often managed to demonstrate, that some very foolish people are in a position to bring the consequences of their folly not only on themselves but on others, we do have the suspicion that something bad is going on. Surely, if we could certainly pronounce certain persons wise, we would think it a good thing to fall under their influence, and it seems only natural and inescapably right to expect some badness from the influence of fools. So it was that I gradually found, in my own considerations of nonsense, less play and more brooding, less glee and more melancholy, and the growing conviction that the silly mind, just as much as the wicked mind, if there is such a thing, makes bad things happen. And my meditations on foolish language, my own included, grew somber and satirical.

Satire is a cunning, landless opportunist who poaches along the borders of the two great realms of Tragedy and Comedy. The hunting is good, no doubt, for the satirist is nourished by folly and vice, of which there is said to be never any shortage. But, perhaps because I was reared in Comedy's fair land, I am not convinced of that. Folly is thick on the ground, no doubt, but where is vice? I know, I truly do know and can demonstrate, just as surely as one can provide a proof in geometry, that certain influential persons, especially in the schools, do bad things to other people. But they are not villains. They do not will badness. On the contrary, probably far more than most of us, they deliberately intend to do good things. And I am certain that they would do good things, if only they could make sense.

But all of that, obviously, could be said of any one of us. Outside of the pages of fantastic fiction, there is no one who says in the heart, I will do evil. We all intend the good, and would, at least often, do it if we could. But we don't always understand what the good is.

That is hardly a new idea. But, while I have known *about* it for a long time, heard it with the hearing of the ear, as it were, I haven't truly *known* it. Between those conditions—knowing about, and knowing—I think there is a very big difference. The point of this book was, for me, the discovery of that understanding. True education is not knowing about, but knowing. It is the cure of folly and the curb of vice, and our only hope of escaping what Socrates once called "the greatest peril of this our life"—not sickness or death, as most of us would say, but the failure to make sense about the better and the worse, and thus to choose the wrong one, thinking it the other.

This is, I'm afraid, a presumptuous book. It is a book about how to live by a man who doesn't know how to live, but who has begun to learn that he doesn't know how.

ONE

Who Is
SOCRATES,
Now That We
NEED HIM?

W HEN BENJAMIN FRANKLIN
was hardly more than a boy, but clearly a comer, he decided
to achieve moral perfection. As guides in this enterprise, he
chose Jesus and Socrates. One of his self-assigned rules for
daily behavior was nothing more than this: "Imitate Jesus
and Socrates."

I suspect that few would disagree. Even most militant
atheists admire Jesus, while assuming, of course, that *they*
admire him for the right reasons. Even those who have no
philosophy and want none admire Socrates, although exactly
why, they can not say. And very few, I think, would tell the
young Franklin that he ought to have made some different
choices: Alexander, for instance, or Francis Bacon.

Jesus, just now, has no shortage of would-be imitators,
although they do seem to disagree among themselves as to
how he ought to be imitated. But the imitators of Socrates,
if any there be, are hard to find. For one thing, if they are
more or less accurately imitating him, they will not organize
themselves into Socrates clubs and pronounce their views. If
we want to talk with them, we will have to seek them out;
and, unless we ourselves become, to some degree at least,
imitators of Socrates, we will not know enough to want to
seek them out. Indeed, unless we are sufficiently his imitators, we might only know enough *not* to want to seek him
out, for some of those who sought Socrates out found reason to wish that they hadn't. Unlike Jesus, or, to be more
accurate, unlike the Jesus whom many imagine, Socrates
often brought not the Good News, but the Bad.

Nevertheless, people do from time to time come to know
enough about Socrates to be drawn into his company, and to
agree, with rare exceptions, that it would indeed be a good
thing to imitate him. The stern poet-philosopher Nietzsche
was one of those exceptions, for he believed, and quite correctly, that reasonable discourse was the weapon with which
the weak might defeat the strong, but most of us often do
think of ourselves as weak rather than strong, and what

seemed a bad thing to Nietzsche seems a good thing to us. However, when we *do* try to imitate Socrates, we discover that it isn't as easy, and as readily possible to millions, as the imitation of Jesus is said to be.

So we make this interesting distinction: We decide that the imitation of Jesus lies in one Realm, and the imitation of Socrates in quite another. The name of the first, we can not easily say, but the name of the second is pretty obviously "mind." Even the most ardent imitators of Jesus seldom think of themselves as imitating the work of his mind, but of, well, something else, the spirit, perhaps, or the feelings, or some other faculty hard to name. But those who would imitate Socrates know that they must do some work in the mind, in the understanding, in the intellect, perhaps even in the formidable "intelligence" of the educational psychologists, beyond whose boundaries we can no more go than we can teach ourselves to jump tall buildings. We may apparently follow Jesus simply by feeling one thing rather than another, but the yoke of Socrates is not easy, and his burden not light, nor does he suffer little children to come unto him.

And we say that, while it would be truly splendid to imitate his example, it really can't be done as a general rule for ordinary life. Very few of us are as smart as Socrates, after all, and the smartest of us are already very busy in computers and astrophysics. Socrates appeared once and only once among us, and the chances of his coming again are very slim. We may hold him up as a shining example, of course, but as a distant star, not a candle in the window of home. He is one in billions. So we must, it seems, resign ourselves to living not the examined life but the unexamined life, responding to the suggestions of environment and the inescapable power of genetic endowment and toilet training.

Nevertheless, millions and millions of us contemplate no serious difficulty at all in imitating the example of Jesus, who, as it happens, is also held to be one in billions. We do *not* say, Ah well, a Jesus comes but once among us, and we lesser folk must content ourselves with remembering, once in a while, some word or deed of his, and trying, although without any hope of truly and fully succeeding, to speak as he might have spoken, to think as he might have thought, and to do as he might have done. Sometimes, to be sure, provided that we do in fact understand him correctly, which is by no means always certain, we might come near the mark. But it is childish and idealistic to imagine that we can, especially in this busiest and most technically demanding of worlds, plainly and simply lived as Jesus lived. No, we do not make those reservations, but suppose rather that, in the case of *this* one life among billions, we can launch ourselves, all at once, and as if by magic, into the Way in which he walked. And this is because we imagine that the Way of Socrates is barricaded by the wall of an intelligence test, and the Way of Jesus is not, that the regularly examined life requires a lot of hard mental labor, and that the good life is as natural and automatic as the singing of the birds.

But there was at least one man who held, and who seems to have demonstrated in a very convincing fashion, that Socrates was not at all special, that he was, indeed, just as ignorant as the rest of us. We can not dismiss him as a political enemy or an envious detractor, or even as a more "advanced" philosopher who had the advantage of modern information to which Socrates had no access. It was Socrates himself who made that demonstration. And, although Plato is surely the most humorous and ironic of philosophers, it is just not possible to read Socrates' *Apology* as a witty trick at the jury's expense. It is a sober autobiography. Socrates explains that he has simply spent his life in trying to discover what the god could have meant in saying, by an astonishing oracle, that Socrates of Athens was the wisest of men. Socrates had discovered, as he had expected, that he knew nothing, but also that the same was true of everybody else. The oracle meant, in effect, that the wisest of men was just as unwise as all other men. But we seem to be fundamentalists about the oracle. There is a curious contradiction in us when we say that Socrates is an inimitable one in billions because of the power of his mind, and thus deny the power of his mind to judge truly as to whether he was an inimitable one in billions. Our minds, which are not up to the work of imitating him, are nevertheless quite strong enough to over-rule him. Strange.

In old age, Franklin admitted that his plan for the achievement of moral perfection had not entirely succeeded, and that he had not, after all, been able perfectly to imitate either Jesus or Socrates. But he did not say that such imitations would have been impossible, or excuse himself from them on the grounds that they would have been impractical or unrealistic, or even, as the modern mind seems very likely to say, that they would have been counterproductive and little conducive to success. He says that, all in all, while he was but an occasional imitator, even so he had thus lived a better and a happier life than he would have otherwise had. And I do suspect that Socrates himself might have said much the same, for he, too, was surely an occasional imitator of Socrates.

The Socrates we have in the dialogues of Plato simply must be a "perfected" Socrates, a masterpiece every bit as much artistic as philosophical. I have lived, and so have you, in this world, which is the very same world in which Socrates lived. Only its temporary particulars have changed. He did, if only when Plato wasn't around, or perhaps before Plato was around, worry about money. He quarreled with his wife, and fell out of patience with his children. He spoke, and even acted, without considering the full meaning and probable consequences of his words and deeds. He even, if only once or twice, saw Reason clearly and completely, and went ahead and listened to Appetite instead. And once in a while, from time to time, he lost his grip on that "cheerful and temperate disposition" without which neither the young nor the old, neither the rich nor the poor, can hope for that decent and thoughtful life of self-government that is properly called Happiness. And such outrageous and unconventional charges I can bring—as can you—against Socrates or anyone, with calm assurance, for Socrates was just a man. To do such things, as he himself very well knew, was merely human.

So now I can see before me one of those persons whom I call, in a very strange manner of speaking, "my" students. There she sits, as close to the back of the classroom as possible. She is blowing bubbles with her gum, and not without skill. She intends to be a schoolteacher. She has read, in their entirety, two books, one about some very frightening and mysterious happenings in a modest suburban house on Long Island, and the other about excellence. I now have reason to hope that she has been reading Emerson, and she probably has. She is not a shirker, but, at least usually, as much a person of serious intent as one should be at her age and in her condition. Her understanding of Emerson is not perfect, but neither is mine. The essay she has been reading, I have read many times, and every time with the realization that my understanding of it, up to now, of course, has not been perfect.

I know this as surely as I know that Socrates was once exasperated by a yapping dog: Someday, perhaps this day, when I have explained some difficult proposition's exploration by Emerson, that young woman, or somebody else very much like her, will raise her hand and ask *the* question, and ask it just as Socrates asked, out of what she knows to be her ignorance, and her desire not to be ignorant. And her question will remind me that I am ignorant, and that I didn't know it, and that I do not want to be.

I probably give less thought than I should to the question of whether the world exists, but I often consider the question of *when* it exists. When I am there in class, considering that young woman's question before me, that is the world. Socrates exists. As though she were Socrates, this blower of bubbles asks the question. She has never thought out or named "undefined terms," "unbounded categories," or "unexamined propositions." She can not *say* that a likeness should be noted where only difference was presumed, or a difference where only a likeness. But she can ask as though she had considered such things. And in that moment, in the world that then and there exists, who is the teacher and who the student? Who is Socrates?

If I have any good sense at all, will I not give *her* question as much thoughtful consideration as I would have given to the same question had it come from Socrates himself? And for two reasons, both of them splendid?

Rather than effectively dismissing Socrates when we suppose that we praise him as "one in billions," we might do better to attend to our words as though we were poets, looking always deeper into and through them. We could thus also say that Socrates is one who is truly *in* billions, the most powerful confirmation that we have of what is, after all, not merely an individual but a generally human possibility—the mind's ability to behold and consider itself and its works. That power is probably unavailable to infants and lunatics, but, in the absence of some such special impediment, who can be without it? Can it be that some of us are empty, and without that power which is the sign of humanity? My bubble-blower certainly is not, and she is real. I have seen her often. And in that moment when she is Socrates, I may well be seeing the first moment of thoughtfulness in her life. Education, real education, and not just the elaborate contraption that is better understood as "schooling," can be nothing but the nourishment of such moments.

I imagine some well-informed and largely wise visitor from another world who comes to Earth to study us. He begins by choosing two people at random, and, since time and place are of no importance to him, but only the single fact of humanity, he chooses Socrates and me, leaving aside for the moment every other human being. He begins with an understanding of the single but tremendous attribute that distinguishes us both from all other creatures of Earth. We are *capable* of Reason. Capable. We *can* know ourselves, unlike the foxes and the oaks, and can know that we know ourselves. He knows that while we have appetites and urges just like all the other creatures, we have the astonishing power of seeing them not simply as the necessary attributes of what we are, but as separate from us in a strange way, so that we can hold them at arm's length, turning them this way and that, and make judgment of them, and even put them aside, saying, Yes, that is "me," in a way, but, when I choose, it is just a thing, not truly *me*, but only *mine*. He sees, in short, what "human" means in "human beings."

And then he considers the specimens he has chosen, Socrates and me. He measures that degree to which they conform to what "human" means in "human beings." With those superior extraterrestrial powers that imagination grants him, he will easily discover:

That I have notions, certain "sayings" in my mind, that flatly contradict one another; believing, for instance, that I can choose for myself the path of my life while blaming other people for the difficulty of the path. With Socrates, this is not the case.

That my mind is full of ideas that are truly nothing more than words, and that as to the meaning of the words I have no clear and constant idea, behaving today as though "justice" were one thing, and tomorrow as though it were another. That, while wanting to be happy and good, I have no clear ideas by which I might distinguish, or might even *want* to distinguish, happiness from pleasure, and goodness from social acceptability. With Socrates, this is not the case.

That I usually believe what I believe not because I have tested and found it coherent and consistent, and harmonious with evidence, but because it is also believed by the right people, people like me, and because it pleases me. And that furthermore, I live and act and speak as though my believing were no different from my knowing. With Socrates, this is not the case.

That I put myself forth as one who can direct and govern the minds, the inner lives, of others, that, in fact, I make my living as one who can do that, but that my own actions are governed, more often than not, by desire or whim. With Socrates, this is not the case.

That I seem to have a great need for things, and think myself somehow treated unjustly by an insufficiency of them, and that this insufficiency, which seems strangely to persist even after I get hold of the thing whose necessity I have most recently noted, prevents in me that cheerful and temperate disposition to which I deem myself entitled. With Socrates, this is not the case.

That I seem to know what I want, but that I have no way of figuring out whether I *should* want what I want, and that, indeed, it does not occur to me that I *should* be able to figure that out. With Socrates, this is not the case.

And that, in short and in general, my mind, the thing that most makes us human, is not doing the steering of this life, but is usually being hustled along on a wild ride by the disorderly and conflicting commands of whole hosts of notions, appetites, hopes, and fears. With Socrates, this is not the case.

How could the alien enquirer help concluding that there is something "wrong" with me, and that the humanness that is indeed in me has been somehow "broken," which he can clearly see by comparing me with Socrates? Must he not decide that Socrates is the normal human, and I the freak, the distortion of human nature?

When he pronounces me the freak, and Socrates the perfectly ordinary, normal human being, living quite obviously, as perhaps only an "alien" can see, by the power of that which most makes a human a human, shall I defend myself by appeal to the principle of majority rule? Shall I say: Well, after all, Socrates is only one human being, and all the others are more like me. Would I not prove myself all the more the freak by my dependence on such a preposterously irrelevant principle? If that visitor were rude, he might well point out that my ability to see, on the one hand, what is natural to human beings, and to claim, on the other, that its absence is only natural, and thus normal, is just the sort of reasoning that he would expect of a freak, whose very freakishness is seen in his inability to do what is simply natural to his species—that is, to make sense.

But Socrates would defend me. He would say, for this he said very often:

No, my young friend is not truly a freak. All that I can do, he can do; he just doesn't do it. And if he doesn't do it, it is because of something else that is natural to human beings, and just as human as the powers that you rightly find human in me. Before we awaken, we must sleep, and some of us sleep deeper and longer than others. It may be, that unless we are awakened by some help from other human beings, we sleep our lives away, and never come into those powers. But we can be awakened.

In that respect, my friend is not a freak. He might better be thought a sleepwalker, moving about in the world, and getting all sorts of things done, often on time, and sometimes very effectively indeed. But the very power of routine habit by which he can do all that has become the only government that he knows. And the voices of his desires are loud. He is just now not in a condition to give his full attention to any meaning that might be found in all that he does, or to consider carefully how to distinguish between the better and the worse. He might be thought a child, and a perfectly natural child, who lives still in that curious, glorious haze of youth, when only desire seems worthy of obedience, and when the mighty fact of the world that is so very "there" looms immeasurably larger than the fact of the self that is in that world. He might grow up, and it is the "mightness" in him that makes him truly human, however he may look like a freak just now. From time to time, we are all just such freaks, and mindless, for mindlessness is the great background of noise out of which some few certain sounds can be brought forth and harmonized as music.

I am often worried and vexed about the colossal social institution of "schooling," of which I am a paid agent. My quarrels and complaint with schooling are beyond my counting, and also, I must admit, valid but trivial. Looming behind all of the silly things that we do in schools, and pass off as an "education" that would have startled Socrates, there is nothing less than a great, pervading spirit of dullness and tedium, of irksome but necessary labors directed completely toward the consolidation of the mundane through the accumulation of the trivial. In school, there is no solemnity, no reverence, no awe, no wonder. We not only fail to claim, but refuse to claim, and would be ashamed to claim that our proper business was with the Good, the True, and the Beautiful, and that this business can be conducted not through arousing pleasant feelings, but through working the mind. Thus it is that education is exceedingly rare in schooling, and when it breaks out, it is as the result of some happy accident, an accident that might have befallen a prepared mind, or maybe any mind at all, just as readily in the streets as in the schools.

Education makes music out of the noise that fills life. And from the random and incessant background noise of what we suppose the "mind," meaning really the appetites and sentiments, education weighs and considers, draws forth and arranges, unites the distant with the near, the familiar with the strange, and makes, by Reason, the harmonious music that *is* Reason. If we can know anything at all about How to

Live, it is in Reason that we must seek it, for the only other possibility is to seek it outside of Reason, in the disorder of noise. I am convinced that Socrates is right, that anyone can make that search and decide, not what the Meaning and Purpose of Life *is*, but what the meaning and purpose of the searcher's life *should* be, and thus to live better.

TWO

The
SQUARE
of the
HYPOTENUSE

WHO FIRST CALLED REASON sweet, I don't know. I suspect that he was a man with very few responsibilities, no children to rear, and no payroll to meet. An anchorite with heretical tendencies, maybe, or the idle youngest son of a wealthy Athenian. The dictates of Reason are often difficult to figure out, rarely to my liking, and profitable only by what seems a happy but remarkably unusual accident. Mostly, Reason brings bad news, and bad news of the worst sort, for, if it is truly the word of Reason, there is no denying it or weaseling out of its demands without simply deciding to be irrational. Thus it is that I have discovered, and many others, I notice, have also discovered, all sorts of clever ways to convince myself that Reason is "mere" Reason, powerful and right, of course, but infinitely outnumbered by *reasons*, my reasons.

Let me give an example. Socrates often considered with his friends a familiar but still vexing question: Which is better, to suffer an injustice or to commit one? He brought them—and me too—to consider the question in some new ways. Which, for instance, is uglier, the person who suffers or the person who commits? Which person has surrendered himself to the *rule* of injustice, and which person might still be able to avoid it? Which might still be free to choose between the better and the worse, and which not? Out of the consideration of such questions, and countless others that flow from them, I know that it is better to suffer an injustice than to commit one just as purely and absolutely as I know about the square of the hypotenuse. If there were some acts possible to me, some ways of living and doing, that could be based in principle on my knowledge of the square of the hypotenuse, what a splendid fellow I would be. In all my dealing with you, and with everybody, I would be strictly on the square. I would no more cut a corner than a right angle would decide, well, just for this once, to enlarge itself by just a little degree or two, which the other angles could surely do without, and which, after all, they might not even

31

notice. Nevertheless, as certain as I am by Reason that suffering injustice is better than doing it, my first reaction to what I consider an injustice done to me is probably just the same as yours. I hate it. I just can't wait to get even. And sometimes, much to my satisfaction, I do. When I do, I call it Justice, not omitting the capital.

So, for some reason with a small "r," I actually find it possible to hate the conclusions of Reason, which would show me that I am all the better off, as well as all the better, for keeping strictly on the receiving end of injustice. From the point of view of Socrates, I guess, I might just as wisely and sanely decide not to go along with the square of the hypotenuse.

I doubt that I could get around Socrates, although I would give it a try, by pointing out that circumstances alter cases, to which he would probably reply, perhaps even with passing reference to that exasperating square of the hypotenuse, that cases don't seem to alter principles, but that, on the contrary, it is precisely because we can detect some underlying principle that we can recognize a case. Nor would I be able to convince him that, in getting even, I had actually done my persecutor a big favor, bringing him to his senses and making him a wiser and better person, which outcome was not really my intention at all. If he had, in fact, been made a better person by my revenge, the credit would not be mine but his, for having managed to find the better in spite of having been dealt the worse. Therefore, on those all-too-rare occasions when I do manage to take a swift and sweet revenge, I don't mention it to Socrates.

Now that is strange behavior, and it is even stranger that it is generally called nothing but "normal" behavior, out of the same presumption, no doubt, that brings us to think Socrates a freak. But lots of people will do just as I do where they find themselves treated, as they see it, unjustly. Lots of those people know every bit as well as I do that Reason does indeed show that it is better to suffer than to do an injustice.

So here we are, they and I, whoever they might be, not only doing what we know to be contrary to the perfectly demonstrable conclusions of Reason, bad enough, but then going on to call that "normal," a lot worse. It is as though we were willing to say that it is normal for human beings, in whom the power of Reason is the quintessential attribute, not only to reject its conclusions but even to despise them. We might just as well say that sanity is, of course, a fine and wholesome condition, but that insanity is normal.

I can not speak for others, but in my own case I find this a vexing conclusion, for when I say that everyone is a little bit crazy, I am surely including myself, a member in standing—"good standing" seems inappropriate at the moment—of the numerous company called "everyone." I do go around in the world putting myself forth as an "educated man," whatever that means. And what can it mean, indeed, if an educated man has to admit, and gladly takes the strange satisfaction that goes with the admission, that he is at least a little bit crazy and just as normal as anyone else who sees Reason but doesn't like it?

It would be one thing if I alone called myself educated, out of some profound misunderstanding of the meaning of education. Then, I could either be set right, or left to my own special craziness. But the fact is that the world also calls me, and countless other people just like me, educated. The world says, in other words: Here is a man who can see some truth and choose not to live by it, a man who excuses himself as normal for giving his feelings and appetites domination over his mind, a man who might actually hate the square of the hypotenuse should it occur to him that his behavior might be circumscribed by the principle it reveals. All of which is to say, here is an educated man.

That already seems to be approaching the preposterous, but the world goes even farther. Here we have one educated man cunningly devising the discomfiture and destruction of his enemies, another cleverly contriving to take possession of the goods of others by force or fraud, and yet another passing out one-way tickets for long rides in boxcars. What sort of definition of education must we have, that we suppose it neither an impediment to immoral behavior nor an imperative to rational behavior?

I am driven, in search of some answer to that question, to compare myself with my unlucky counterpart, the uneducated man. Here he stands, the poor ignoramus, knowing neither Dante nor Debussy. He has never heard of Socrates or of syllogisms. He can neither write a grammatical sentence nor read one. He is not impelled to meditation by the square of the hypotenuse, and he wouldn't for a minute swallow any of that nonsense about putting up with injustice. Ah, how different we are. He watches reruns of "Laverne and Shirley," and I stick to "Masterpiece Theater" and "Nova." He and his pals, furthermore, outnumber me and mine enormously. No wonder the world is always in such a mess.

I find myself feeling sorry for him, and imagining how much better a person he might have been had he only spent more of his life paying close attention, and some fees, to people like me. I am, after all, a teacher. Have I not pledged myself to make people better? What a pity it is that this poor slob never put himself under my instruction and learned to be better, like me. Ah, well, we can't all be that lucky, and, after all, somebody does have to do all the hard and messy work that I am too educated to do.

And how lucky I am that he is probably rather inarticulate. And I do hope that he remains inarticulate, lest he say what I should hear:

So, I would be better would I, if I were more like you, eh? Do you mean that I too would then be able to recognize and coherently describe the conclusions of Reason before I reject them and decide to do as I please? Is that what you teach in your school—how to go beyond an unknowing obedience to appetite into a fully conscious and willful obedience to appetite? Do you have the brass, Jack, to tell me that it is better to know the good and to refuse it than to be ignorant of the good—as you suppose me— and to miss it? The important differences between us that I can see are that you choose to be irrational and I can't help being irrational, and that you have been rewarded for the cleverness out of which you do that choosing with a handsome collection of diplomas.

Yes, diplomas. About that, at least, he's surely right. I do have all sorts of information that he lacks. I know the kings of England, and I quote the fights historical, although I must admit that I'm no longer sure of the cheerfulness of those many facts about the square of the hypotenuse. Of course, he might also have lots of information that I lack, but the kind of information he has is...well...a different kind of information, you know. Not quite as classy. It's about how to do some sort of work, perhaps, or maybe about baseball statistics or something. It's not that *educated* kind of information that I have.

Still, the difference does seem to be a matter of information, and, of course, diplomas, which are testimonials to the fact that some other people with lots of the "educated kind" of information were willing to concede that I had acquired some sufficient amount of that too. And, thinking of that, a strange and unnerving thought strikes me. It's not as easy as I thought to define that educated kind of information. Socrates and Aquinas were also utterly ignorant of Dante and Debussy, and they didn't watch any television at all, not even "Masterpiece Theater." They never read Dostoyevski or Kant, and they never even heard of calculus or quantum mechanics. (I, of course, am informed about those two mysteries, which is to say, needless to say, that I *have* heard of them.) And Socrates never read Aquinas, who did, at least, read Plato, and especially Aristotle, whom Socrates also never read. But it would be very hard, even for me, educated as I am, to deny such minds the rank, if rank it is, of "educated."

On the other hand, I suspect, no, I know, that they would not admit me to that rank. They shared, across many centuries, an idea about education, and about its absolute dependence on Reason rather than information, that we do not share. I'm not so sure about Aquinas, for he was a schoolman, after all, but Socrates cared nothing for schools or diplomas. Both, however, understood that education had no necessary relationship to schools or diplomas, and both held that the true goal of education was to make people able to be good.

I think it's important to put it just that way—*able* to be good. That phrase contains some remarkable suggestions. We do suppose that the aim of education is to make people able to do some sort of work, to be engineers or physicians or social workers or something else, and we do hope that as many of them as possible will be good at what they do. But by that, we mean "effective." And we are pretty clear about what it is that will make them effective—some combination of talent, information, and practice, producing, of course, some visible and measurable results in the world that we all can see. But Socrates and Aquinas would not want us to confuse any person's effectiveness, his skill in his calling, with his Goodness, quite another thing.

But that's a fairly elementary suggestion of "able to be good." It also suggests that being good is not, as it often seems, and as it surely pleases us to believe, a matter of temperament and character, combined with suitable feelings, and maybe a little bit of luck. It is, rather than a skill, a power and a propensity, both of which can be learned and consciously applied.

I do have some practical experience of the fact that lots of people find that notion either just plain silly or astonishing. I often ask my students to read at least some parts of Benjamin Franklin's autobiography, and there, as I intended, they soon come to that passage in which Franklin describes his youthful ambition to achieve moral perfection. So how hard could it be? He knew, after all, the roots of moral failure, a mix of custom, bad company, and his own weaknesses, and felt that, by knowing them for what they were, and by a deliberate act of will, he would certainly be able to pay them strict attention and to keep them all under control.

He made a little chart, the sort of thing on which my earliest piano teacher, and yours too, I imagine, used to stick little stars in recognition of some slight improvement in arpeggios. Franklin's chart was a list of virtues to be practiced every day, and every evening he gave himself grades. It is a bit Eagle Scoutish, and the whole idea seems bizarre to my students, and that for at least two very important reasons. First, they do not see any reason to call patience "better" than impatience, but only different, and second, because even if patience were for some unaccountable reason to be thought the better, those who don't have it, just don't have it, and that's the way it is. To them, an impatient person is impatient in the same way that a left-handed person is left-handed, and trying to make some change in the first case might be, for all they know, as dangerous and disabling as enforcing change in the second. They don't see, at first, that patience, even if it can be understood as a virtue, is something that anyone can *do* anything about.

Socrates, and Franklin too, would have remarked on the extraordinary convenience of that belief. But, in fairness to my students, it is not because of its convenience that they have come into that belief, nor did they choose it. It was, in fact, thrust upon them, like so many other ideas that they don't notice that they have. Indeed, it doesn't take more than a little discussion, salted with just the right questions, to bring them—well, quite a few of them—to see just how convenient a belief it is, and to wonder, a bit suspiciously, just how they came to believe it in the first place. And then, the conscious and deliberate practice of patience seems less bizarre, and not dangerous. Perhaps, even, "good," whatever that means.

This invariable result—it truly never fails—convinces me that an ancient idea of the meaning of education is a better one than whatever it is we now assume. It says first that if we can know the Good, it is by the power of Reason; and second, that there is in all of us a hunger for the Good, so that, as Reason little by little seems to reveal it, we are delighted and enthralled. It is as though we were hearing, at last, what we have always longed to hear, without having any idea at all what it was. My students still see Franklin's chart as—well, overoptimistic, to say the least, as Franklin himself saw it from the distance of many years, but they also see that it is based on an idea that makes some sense, and that can be known. They see, furthermore, that to this idea they were, for some strange reason, simply blind. They just hadn't thought of it, nor had anyone proposed it for them.

They see, too, and I think this a terribly important realization, that they are perfectly capable of understanding it, and that their understanding has nothing to do with having taken the right courses and having gotten good grades, and nothing to do, either, with the so-called lessons of experience. Experiences they have surely had, but it is only now, in the light of some hitherto unsuspected principle, that those experiences can suddenly be construed as lessons.

My students do, I'm sure, put all of that out of their minds the next day. And why shouldn't they? So does their teacher. Having discussed Franklin's ideas about the practice of patience on Tuesday, their teacher gets in his car on Wednesday and rushes across the nearest bridge, carefully switching from lane to lane lest he find himself in any tollbooth line but the shortest. Then, ending up behind some woman driver who *thought* she had exact change, he curses the inexorable destiny that seems to follow him everywhere, and the folly of a government that gives driving licenses to women.

But they do not forget forever. Someday, somewhere, the idea reappears, at least in many of them. It has a quality that schoolwork often lacks. It is seductive, enticing, it will not leave the mind alone. I know this not only from their testimony, but from my own experience, when I do happen to consider experience in the light of principle. From time to time, while fuming in the tollbooth line, I do think of Franklin's chart. I am, to be sure, rebuked, but also enticed; troubled, but also consoled.

Those are attributes of true education, but the enticement and the consolation do not begin to appear until the rebuke has been delivered and the troubling begun. Socrates was well acquainted with that unpleasant onset, the first stirring not unlike a small and suspiciously unfamiliar pain in the belly that tells you that you may be in for big trouble. He was speaking of people who had no philosophy and wanted none, meaning by "philosophy" not the elaborate and esoteric discipline that we have instituted in our schools, but only a certain way of the mind, a certain habitual resort to Reason, and a certain propensity to talk about Goodness. Such people, he said, if only they will stay around and hear an argument out, begin to get a little twitchy. They are vexed by something that they know they don't like, but without knowing why they don't like it. They want to object, but they know not how.

They are like people who discover, on first hearing about the square of the hypotenuse, that something or other about it does not please them. But they can hardly say, No, no, it isn't that way at all! So they brood. They go away at last, discontented, and unable, at least for a while, to return to their former states of well-being. Some, of course, will never come back for another session of the mental equivalent of root canal. But some will.

Nevertheless, even those who come back also go away again. And that is why I am always so ready to take revenge. I know better, but I don't do better. That is not a good condition, not a condition of Goodness. However, there is a yet worse condition. I would be in worse condition if I did not know that I am in bad condition. That worse condition, whatever its proper name, must be *the* condition out of which education can lead us.

The word "education" does suggest some process that leads outward, and its best opposite would be a word we don't have, "induction," a leading inward. The idea of liberation suggests a great metaphor, a picture of a place, the Waiting Room of the Mind, perhaps even the Prison Camp of the Mind, out of which, someday, somehow, the mind might be led, or in which it might languish, or even, worst of all, in which it might be forever held captive.

I must see myself, then, as one at the door of the waiting room, one in whom the enterprise worthy of the name of education has only begun. I have come out of something, but I haven't come very far out of it. There is more outing to be done. How shall I do it? How shall I even learn to *want* to do it, for I am, I must confess, very reluctant to give up the delicious pleasures (as I now find them) of such things as revenge and just complaint against women who imagine, contrary to all experience and common sense, that they can find three quarters in their purses.

I would like to say, of course, since that would at least make the enterprise seem easier, that "mere" Reason, by itself, will not lead me out. That, after all, is what the world says, and it is, like my students' automatic belief that nothing can or should be done about perfectly natural endowments like patience or impatience, a remarkably convenient belief. I often wish that I could share that convenient belief but to do so would be to conclude, and to claim, that I have already done everything that the power of reason permits, which I haven't. I have done only enough to see, but from a distance, some better condition into which reason might yet bring me. I can not yet say, therefore, that Reason will not lead me out. I don't know that. I have heard others saying it, as we all have, but that is not the same as knowing it, knowing it for and in myself.

Education, I am convinced, must be nothing more than this: The journey toward the limits of Reason, if any there be. And if any there be, so that some other and even better condition than education may lie beyond them, we can hardly hope to enter into the greater mystery without passing through the lesser.

If I have come but a short way on that journey, diplomas notwithstanding, I would like to pass at least some of the blame for that to induction, a vast and diverse condition of life, ordinarily as impalpable to us as air was to our ancient ancestors. Induction, in terms probably much too simple to be entirely accurate, but good enough, I hope, for now, includes all the forces and influences that, whether by accident or design, make it difficult for us to think clearly. There is no counting of them. Some of them are in us, and some outside, in the very air we breathe, as it were, and those inside we exhale into the world where they afflict others with clouded thinking, thus making the air we breathe what it is. All of those forces and influences, we made, for there is in the whole universe, as far as we can tell, no other thinking creature, and thus, happily, I suppose, no other misthinking creature.

We are all born in captivity. That is no disgrace, for there is no other place in which to be born. Without the nurture of all the rest of our kind, we do not become our kind. We need captivity. But, unlike the other animals, whose original endowment is also their ultimate endowment, we can be born, as it were, in one world, and come at last to live in quite another. By our nature we can do something that no other creature we know of is able to do. The equivalent act in an oyster would be to discover that it lives in the sea, and not in

41

the jungle; and that it *is* an oyster, and not some other creature; and that it is only *the* oyster that it is, and unique; and that its countless and complicated natural functions, taken all together, do not quite add up to its *self*.

When we make the equivalent discoveries, we see that there is one world of We and another of I. From the latter, an "I" can behold and consider the former, but it doesn't work the other way around.

THREE

The
LAND
of
WE ALL

ONE OF THE FIRST FACTS about thinking seems too obvious to be worth mentioning, but, it isn't always obvious, and we often behave as though it weren't a fact. Only a person can think. I don't mean by that to point out that trees and rocks can't think, but to say, rather, that even if trees and rocks could think, only *a* tree or *a* rock could think. Thinking can not be done corporately. Nations and committees can't think. That is not only because they have no brains, but because they have no selves, no centers, no souls, if you like. Millions and millions of persons may hold the same thought, or conviction or suspicion, but each and every person of those millions must hold it all alone. And that it truly is the same thought in all of them, the very same thought, each must guess of all the others, for into each other's minds we can not get. All I can ever know of what you think is your testimony, which may well be as inexpert or self-interested as mine often is. Every thinker is unique, since every person is unique.

From a certain point of view, thinking is preposterous behavior, and astonishing. If its appearance among us is truly the result of some evolutionary "save-the-species" development, it is clearly one of Nature's great mistakes, for it, and it alone, has made of us the only species not only able to destroy itself, but very likely to destroy itself. Of course, I might have that wrong if it is really in Nature's great plan to save all the other species by planting in the most dangerous one a lethal seed, but that requires in Nature a low cunning which seems beneath her. In any case, however, it is perfectly clear that other creatures do very well indeed without thinking, without seeking the meaning of their deeds, without making and testing propositions, and without reading or writing. All such acts, and countless related ones, from the point of view of all the rest of the universe that we know of, must be accounted nothing but "unnatural."

In thinking about thinking, and in thinking about anything, for that matter, it is always useful to think about something else instead. Give some thought to the playing of the violin. Imagine that some great team of skilled researchers has given itself to, and at last accomplished, a study of violin-playing, a detailed and comprehensive description of absolutely everything that is happening in a human being who is playing the violin. Their work has been tremendous, and their findings occupy a whole shelf, maybe a whole wing, for their considerations begin at least at the submolecular level of neural signals, and reach, at the far end of some unimaginably long line, all those things that we vaguely point to when we talk about the imagination and understanding of the artist. And all such things the researchers have weighed and measure and counted.

Imagine now the immensely distant future, when we have ceased on the Earth, and when there are no singers, no songs, and no violin-playing. Visitors from another world arrive, and find some few remnants, among them, the great, exhaustive study of violin-playing, complete with pictures and charts and tables of figures, to say nothing of ear-witness accounts of the feat itself. Will they not be astonished, and reach pretty much the same conclusion that even you and I would reach should we be able to read such a study? Will they not say: This is too much. Any fool can see that the playing of the violin is simply impossible.

When such a task is seen in all of its details, it takes on the look not only of the impossible, but even of the unnatural. To one who considers all of the great and harmonious workings of Nature, the deep and continual principles that inform them, all that might be called not only Order but even The Order, nothing could seem more contrary and unlikely than that a person should bring forth ravishing beauty from a dinky wooden box.

But in fact, as anyone can see, that is only one of countless unlikely things that persons do. And thinking is another such. If the great study of violin-playing would fill a whole wing, the great study of thinking would need a few libraries all to itself. But it can be done. And—an even more startling fact—it can be done by a person who can also play the violin.

Playing the violin or writing a poem are special ways of paying attention. They are acts at once small and great. Although only one person can commit them, they require orderly marshallings of countless and diverse forces, something like the great landing of armies in Normandy, but incalculably bigger and more complicated. And such a comparison leads to another important clue in thinking about thinking. Playing the violin, and thinking, and landing in Normandy are indubitably human accomplishments, for better or worse, in either case. But they are accomplishments very different in nature, for while human beings, and only human beings, can achieve them all, only an individual person can achieve the playing and the thinking, both of which are the more difficult, and complicated, and unlikely. The great study of the invasion can in fact be written, and even read. It was. But the great study of violin-playing will never be done.

It is an obvious but simple distinction—though rarely made—that there are some things that we can do because we are humanity, and some things that we can do because we are persons, and that there is some radical and absolute difference between the two classes of things. They do not overlap. A person can no more invade Normandy than an army can play the violin. Furthermore, while the deeds that pertain to humanity are frequently very large and very visible, so that we can all see just how stupendous they are, and the deeds that pertain to persons seem very small and are often utterly invisible; it takes only a little reflection to conclude that the latter are far greater accomplishments than the former, beggaring description and final analysis, and, at last, unlikely.

But the deeds of humanity are given, in our minds, a superiority over the deeds of persons. By contrast with the waging of war, the playing of the violin seems immensely less important, a trifle, in fact. It is an interesting opinion, for its validity depends entirely on what meaning we are to take from the word "important." It isn't true, of course, that Nero fiddled while Rome burned, and I don't know what meaning I would take from the fact if he had, but if Oistrakh had fiddled through the siege of Leningrad, as Dame Myra played Mozart through the Blitz, I would see a person doing one sort of thing and humanity doing another sort of thing, and I would wonder about what I might learn to mean by the word important.

About this I don't have to wonder: Dame Myra, or Oistrakh, or perhaps even Nero, for all I know, could also have wondered about what they might mean by the word important, but humanity could not. Humanity does not wonder. Only a person can wonder. And the list is very long of verbs that can be added to the words "Only a person..." If you will make yourself such a list of verbs, and then another of the verbs that go with "Only humanity can..." you will discover a lot of things to wonder about, and one of the more important ones will be the meaning that you might learn to assign to the word important.

While it may well be that few persons ever happen to notice and consider the strange and unique powers that they have as persons, and not as humanity, including the power to decide what important should mean, I suspect that we all have some inkling of that strange state of affairs. That is why we are warned in schools—well, maybe in some schools—against what is generally called "generalization." Generalizations often name many minds and then go on to speak as though they were *a* mind. Right from the start, they speak of what is not, for the Italians can not believe one thing and the Belgians another. Only a person can believe, or think—or feel, for that matter. And when we undertake to talk about what is not, we are in danger of falling into nonsense and talking rubbish.

But the warning against generalization is ordinarily provided not for intellectual reasons but for social reasons. It is certainly true that vague generalization provides an easy way to insult lots of people all at once without having to prove anything, but it also provides an easy way to praise or flatter lots of people all at once without having to prove anything. If I say that Jews are stingy, I will be accused first of some social depravity, and only thereafter, and rarely, too, of intellectual disorder. Furthermore, my intellectual disorder, speaking as though Jews were an agent who could *be* stingy, will be at least partially excused should I back off a bit and say, to what will surely be general assent, Well, some Jews are stingy. Who can deny it? Some Eskimos are also stingy. I will not be required to specify a percentage.

Having corrected myself socially, I will not be required to correct myself intellectually. And I will suffer no correction at all if I say that Jews are diligent and productive. Now, I am OK, and listeners will nod approvingly. Nor will I be required to say, even approximately, how many Jews are diligent and productive, or which ones.

In one of the worlds in which I live, the World of We All, the first assertion is a Bad Thing, and the second a Good Thing. But in another world in which I also live, the world where the mind does its work, the two statements are perfectly equal in value, and their value is zero. They are worthless statements. It is not sufficient to condemn them as generalizations, for that condemnation is really an exoneration as well. The most we require of a generalization is that it be toned down. Come on, now, they can't *all* be stingy. And when we declaw our generalizations, we suppose that we have come out of the Wrong and into the Right. But we have only come out of one worthlessness and into another.

There are several ways by which to detect a worthless statement. One of them is making it into its opposite, and considering the statement and its supposed negation side by side. The opposite of a worthless statement is always worthless. If we test the proposition that fat men are jolly by asserting also that fat men are morose, we do not notice that light has been shed on the ordinarily expectable disposition of fat men. Neither proposition suggests any possibility of verification or of falsification. We can not ask, If the first were true, what else would be true? We can not look for evidence for the support of the one or the other, because we can not find, in the world, the real *subject* of either sentence, as we could if the subject were something like a cannonball dropped from a leaning tower, or a certain fat man well known to us. We can not find "fat men." At what weight will we set our definition? Will we omit some men who fall short by three ounces? Will we include those who were three ounces too skinny in the morning but somehow manage to satisfy us as fat after lunch? And what will we do about jolly, and morose? Or stingy and productive, for that matter? Where will we set their limits? How closely will be able to measure them?

Worthless statements can thus be understood as propositions that we simply can not use for thinking. They just don't work. It is not because they are mysteries or concepts that transcend thought, like the nature and substance of the Holy Ghost, or circularity in the absence of circles, but because they do not rise to the level of thought, in which we find that we need to make meaningful statements about meaningful statements.

Worthless statements are a kind of social grace, except, of course, when they are a social disgrace. They have, in the work of the mind, the same value as, Well, it's good to see you. How have you been? But, at their worst, which is where they usually roost, they are dangerous deceptions of the mind. They leave us, if we are not attentive, with the vague impression that we know something, when we don't, thus providing us with the chance of going on to suppose that we know something else as a consequence of something that we don't know. No good is likely to come of that, except by the happiest accident, and for harm to come of it requires no accident at all. This is especially true in that part of life which is social, for it is exactly there, where great masses of people are made into the subjects of propositions, that the worthless statement most flourishes, with predictable consequences.

I have been reading, over and over for a few years now, a piece I tore out of a newspaper. It is a quotation from a book, and it was printed alongside a review of the book, as an example of good work. The reviewer did not like the book. The author seems to be a decent and energetic woman who gave up a successful career as a physician to devote herself to what is perhaps an even higher calling. She is dismayed, as I am too, by the prospect, perhaps the likelihood, of an unimaginably destructive nuclear war. She now devotes her life to arousing others to the danger of the threat, and the book in question is part of her work to that end.

I am on her side. I suspect that I would like her. She is, in principle, saying a very fine thing: Come, let us reason together. This represents exactly that sort of education I think is the only true one, an education in Reason—that work of the mind by which we can, if it can be known, know the Good. And know the evil too, and see it for what it is, and turn away from it. If we can not save ourselves from nuclear destruction by the work of the mind, then our future will be just a matter of luck, and where war is concerned, we seem little likely to be lucky. But if it is the work of the mind that will save us, then the work of the mind badly done will destroy us, unless, again, we are lucky. Read now what she says and consider whether the mind's work in this case be done well or ill:

It is true that we have the secret of atomic energy locked in our brains forever. But this does not mean that we can't alter our behavior. Once we practiced slavery, cannibalism, and dueling; as we became more civilized, we learned

51

that these forms of behavior were antithetical to society, so we stopped. Similarly, we can easily stop making nuclear weapons, and we can also stop fighting and killing each other.

In trying to keep your mind clear, it is always a good idea to be on the lookout for the pronoun "we." If "fat men" make up a category too big and shapeless for us to say anything accurate about, we is clearly much larger, and, unfortunately, not at all shapeless. Except where some defined context limits it to exactly these or those of us, we has to be all of us. Every one. And people who make moral propositions have a way of talking about we, and making thus the same kind of worthless statement that I can make by talking about fat men.

And, because we is everybody, it is nobody. It is simply not a person, not a center of consciousness that can think and feel and do, and is therefore capable of no one of those acts named by the verbs that go with the statement "Only a person can . . ."

I am *bona fide* member of we. So are you. About you I can not speak, but for myself I can say, and not at all to my shame, that I have never given up slavery. I have never even dreamed of it. If you are depending, for the sake of the survival of our species, on the fact that I have learned to alter my behavior and have thus forsworn slavery, then you are leaning on a weak reed, and the future of our species is not bright. Nor do I suspect for a minute that I am just one of the die-hards, still holding fast to the practice of slavery when almost everyone else has learned better. I rather suspect that, among we, there are actually billions like me, who have never given up slavery, having had, like me, no reason to do so, having never, just like me, practiced it in the first place. I suspect, furthermore, and the history of an especially bloody war leads me to that suspicion, that many who did give up slavery, did it not out of some moral reawakening, but under duress—that is to say, not as a result of what a person can do, but as a result of what humanity can do. Their giving up was an outer event, and not an inner act. And I have to wonder about the author of that passage. Did she have some inner reason to give up slavery? And did she proceed, by a conscious and supremely important act of the will, to give it up?

If we now look around at all of our species, and flatter ourselves as persons who have learned at least enough goodness to grant our slaves their freedom, we say what is not so. Somewhere in North Africa or the deep jungles of Borneo, it may be possible to find a chieftain or two who has in fact done exactly that, but I think it unlikely that we can depend on them to save us from war.

I will have to say the same about dueling and cannibalism. I have never given them up. In those respects, I am not the better person implied in that we. And there is very probably hardly anyone who is. Where will we find all of those people who, having learned better how to order society and become better persons, will now be the better persons who stop fighting and killing each other?

Any proposition has two sides. It always says, in its simplest form, that A is B. The A of those propositions simply doesn't exist. There surely have been people who did once give up those wicked practices, but they are gone from us. Could they hear us boasting that *we* made those decisions, they might be a bit put out. Perlman might do little more than raise an eyebrow if I were to claim that we had learned to play the violin, but the heroes of Marathon might actually turn nasty if I were to boast that we found on that little beach the strength and determination to turn back the stronger force of tyranny. The B's of those propositions, however, do indeed exist. And, if we can understand them not just by their titles but by their principles, it may become clear that practically *no one* has ever given them up.

Here is another way in which our language can trick us

53

into imagining that we are thinking. The names of things are not the things, and we have many names that point to no things at all, but to ideas. What is slavery? In one sense, it is easily identified. Where one person is allowed to have, by law, possession of another person, ownership, with all the rights that traditionally go with ownership, that is slavery. In our own nation, that law was changed, but not by those who owned the slaves. As to whether those who made the change sought the moral betterment of those who resisted it, or something else, there is at least room for speculation.

But what is the root of slavery? What is it *in principle*, rather than in detail? How did such a practice come to be established by humanity, and, apparently, universally established at that? Here, there is room for both speculation and introspection. Which of us can say that he has never used another person as though that person were an object? Which of us has resisted every impulse to control or govern another? Which of us has never deemed himself better and more valuable than another? Which of us has never sought to put some fence around the mind of another? Is there one of us who has not thought what even Plato thought, that there are certain people who are—well, just inferior, by nature, just not capable of living under their own direction, and that we are actually doing them a favor by directing their lives for them, in some way or another?

I will plead guilty to all of those charges, and I would be very eager to meet a person who is innocent of them all, for then I might best study Goodness. But, thinking not in terms of laws and social conventions, which are always changing, and for reasons that have nothing to do with Goodness, but only with Necessity, I will have to admit again, but for a very different reason, that I have not given up slavery, for indeed, I still practice it.

I can be very specific about that. I can, and do, so overpower the minds of my students, those, at least, who want to pay attention, and who have little defense, that they come to believe what I seem to believe, to judge as I judge. When that happens, I have to start contradicting myself, and pointing to the uncertainties of my own reasoning, until they too come around to the new course, and the process begins again. Is the root of slavery not in them as well as in me? Who of us has not sought to be led? Which of us has not, from time to time, abandoned the difficult task of understanding for ourselves, of governing ourselves, even of supporting ourselves? Which of us has not wanted a master, so that we might be as well taken care of as a puppy, fed and watered and cleaned up after? Why is it that my students, when they come to be entirely of my mind, think that that is what they are *supposed* to do? What taught them that, if not some cultivation and even some encouragement in them of whatever it is in us all that fears the perils of freedom? And the cultivators and encouragers, or even the permitters— have they given up slavery?

Nor have I given up dueling. I still duel. I still seek to avenge my "honor." I still incline to answer fire with fire, and injustice, whatever I mean by that, with justice, whatever I mean by *that*. That I do not go out at dawn with pistols is not enough to save me from the name of duelist.

On cannibalism, I will make a small concession. While I never did give it up, I have also never knowingly practiced it. It is, in any case, not at all the same sort of "crime" or "depravity" as slavery or dueling, or even as fighting and killing, not rooted in what may well be some permanent and universal facts about human beings. We do know that it was usually practiced only as a religious ritual, and we also know that our supposed innate abhorrence of cannibalism disappears quite readily under the clear and imminent threat of starvation, as survivors of airplane crashes in the high mountains will testify. But cannibalism, too, might well have been "given up" by some person or persons who did indeed come into some new moral understanding. Where are they now? What role will they have to play in the moral reawakening by which we will all escape the coming storm?

If you were to ask the next three persons you meet in the street to give a few reasons for the fact that so many people seem unable to think coherently, consistently, and logically, you would hear some obvious answers. Some of those answers would refer to what is called "intelligence." Well, some people are just smarter than others, and thus naturally capable of more and better thought. You would hear answers about something called "judgment," and very likely accompanied by the complaint that the schools just don't teach judgment anymore, as though they always had, of course, in the good old days when everyone was consistently able to think coherently. Your most sophisticated informant might well point to the notorious difficulty of strict and formal logic, which the schools also don't teach anymore. After all, are there not dozens and dozens of those syllogisms, each with a name of its own, and each indispensable to clear and correct thought? Just think of all those famous fallacies, and how easily the untrained mind will stumble into them. And then, of course, there is ignorance, in this context to be strictly construed not as dullness of mind, but as the simple absence of information, and thus a widespread impediment to clear thinking even in the smartest. And just think how much information there is! Who could have it all, or even any considerable share of it?

There is some usefulness in all of those understandings, but they seem to me quite unable to explain the thinking we have been considering here. The author of those thoughts on slavery remains, whether she practices or not, a skillful physician. She must indeed be what we call "smart," and diligent as well. Her profession requires logical thought, and lots of it, and the drawing of correct inferences from the evidence of knowable facts, a process which must be granted the rank of judgment. I would put the care of my body under her supervision with no misgivings at all, knowing that where she had knowledge she would act effectively, and that where she had not enough knowledge, she would know that she had not enough knowledge, and send me to someone who did.

Nor would I say, of the thoughts we have been thinking about, that she has wandered "out of her field." There are some people who do put themselves forth as experts in the mysteries of the human heart and soul—all sorts, from psychiatrists and economists to preachers and politicians—but those mysteries are, and in fact *should* be, everybody's field. Who are you, who am I, who is *anybody*, to be disqualified as to that inquiry? If there is any special expertise to be had in contemplating human mysteries and speaking what truth can be had about them, it might be in our poets and dramatists and novelists, or even in our myths and music, but who surely knows which? No, we are not dealing here with someone who is just out of her depth in a highly technical subject. The impediments to her clear thinking are not to be found in any of the answers given above. They come from pains in her belly.

The Greeks supposed that the belly was the nursery and dwelling place of the appetites and desires, just as they supposed that the head was the home of thought, and the chest the place of right feelings, a reasonable mediation between the two. Their knowledge of anatomy would not have gotten them through our medical schools, but their metaphor provides powers of the mind that are not instilled in our medical schools, or any other. That metaphor has this great virtue, that it gives us the beginning of a way to distinguish internal and invisible events from one another by family, as it were. We can be almost as clear in our minds about the different denizens of the belly, the chest, and the head, as we can about animals, vegetables, and minerals.

(I am thinking just now, as many readers may know, about a long essay by C. S. Lewis, "Men Without Chests." It is about what seems to Lewis a general and growing inability either to dethrone or harmonize technical information or prowess and gut feelings. It is good to read. Once a year.)

Consider again that, even in the company of those we call "intellectuals," I would suffer rebuke or disapproval in saying that Jews are stingy, and escape both in saying that Jews are diligent and productive. As thinking, both statements are equal. Both worthless. If I can get away with the second, even in lofty mental company, it is because what I say probably makes every belly in the room purr with satisfaction, while the first makes them all growl with unease.

Of course, it may be a bit more complicated than that. Some belly may be in spasm, truly pleased to hear Jews called stingy, but fearful lest its owner be revealed as bigoted. That owner will very likely permit his belly its secret pleasure and send his head forth to do a little socially acceptable lying. I will still get the rebuke and disapproval. To escape it, and thus get away with an utterly worthless proposition, all I have to do is make the bellies purr. Lots of people know that secret, and live very well by it indeed.

The passage cited earlier will make many bellies purr. There are probably very few people who are looking forward to nuclear war, and thus anxious about all the rest of us who are hoping to find some way to prevent it. Who but a maniac out of an old-fashioned science-fiction novel would contemplate with glee the destruction of all life, or even of lots of it? Who would not lament the destruction of the butterflies, which is actually, and just a little bit unfortunately, one of the hideous possibilities used by the author in her "argument"?

But if it is by reasoning together that we may escape nuclear war, then her thinking may kill us all. In that marvelously pliable land of we all, anybody can get away with anything. Her opponents, and there must be some, for otherwise there could be no threat, can write books claiming that we have learned, through bitter lessons, that force succumbs only to force, and that we have thus given up, or certainly should give up, our childish dreams of perpetual peace. Just as cogently as she, which is to say, not at all, but with just as much hope of making bellies purr, others can say that we have learned that the price of freedom is supreme sacrifice, and thus given up the belief, which might also be called "antithetical to civilization," that we can enjoy its fruits without paying its costs.

There is lots of talk these days about "teaching children to think," a presumed function of the schools, which they are either executing well or ill, depending on which expert speaks. Of what can that teaching of thinking consist, I wonder. What exercises can be done? Are the answers in the back of the book, or only in the teachers' manual? What would I do, if I had to teach children to think?

The first thing I would do, I hope, would be to get out of the land of we all, and recognize that "children" do not con-stitute an entity capable of thought. So I would set out to discover how to teach *a person* to think. And, since the task seems formidable, I would prefer, for my first try at such work, to pick the person myself, one who shows some promise. And I would pick, of course, a person who says that we have given up slavery and dueling and cannibalism.

And where would I begin, with a person who is already, as we understand the term, not only "educated," but "highly educated"? With the belly, of course, which in this case has overpowered the head. The greatest failures of thinking do not come from any incapacities of the mind, nor are they prevented by great skills of the mind. They come from the interference emitted by the feelings, which can be both de-tected and disarmed by the one great power of thought that is the mother of all others, and that is self-knowledge, the beginning of all thoughtfulness.

FOUR

The
RIGHT
Little
THING

THERE IS A STORY ABOUT THE importance of self-knowledge in the Fourth Gospel, but I think it is traditionally misunderstood because of certain disorders of the belly, some feelings that are little examined because they are generally thought to be simply "right." One of the those feelings, of course, is that Jesus ought not to be included in the company of those who were merely Great Teachers, such as Socrates and Confucius. They were all proponents of self-knowledge, of course, but Jesus.... Well, he may have thought self-knowledge a good thing, but he really set his sights far higher, we say, and had some greater sort of knowledge in mind. And, since many will assert that *that* knowledge is not truly a work of the mind, but of something else, you could probably get yourself in a great deal of trouble in some company by saying that Jesus was a supremely educated man who undertook to lead others in the paths of education. But I will have to take that risk, and say further that he urged an education that begins, and ends, in self-knowledge.

He was surely a stern teacher, who knew when to rebuke the ignorance of self. What's wrong with you people? he said. When the wind blows from the South, you know that the day will be hot; and when it blows from the East, you know enough to prepare for the coming storm. So how come you can't read the signs in yourselves? And in the famous story of the woman caught in adultery, known even to unbelievers, he can be seen setting the model for that enterprise that we now find so necessary and so difficult: Teaching the Children to Think.

What a strange and wonderful story that is. Behold their dire approach, the righteous men who have caught a naughty girl in the very act, a posse of vigilantes, we usually think. And up to cunning tricks as well, for we see them setting a trap for Jesus. All right, Mister Master, what about this? You know the Law, and you know what has to be done in this case just as well as we do. So how are you going to wriggle out of this one, with all your sweet talk of forgiveness and mercy? What a poser. And isn't it just like them, those unregenerate, stiff-necked Pharisees?

But wait. Is it the mind or the belly that paints that portrait? Are they not citizens doing what they do believe, and what all their society presumably believes, their civic duty as well as their religious duty? Are they not charged with the deed they intend, just as we are charged, both by law and whatever we mean by morality, to report our knowledge of crime? And do they not respect that charge, as we do, finding it both worthy and necessary for the orderly life of us all? Therefore, whether adultery can be accounted a crime or not according to *our* law, is not the point; it is the obedience to law that matters.

Do we see those men as cruel vigilantes because we are good democrats, on the side of the woman, weak and alone against the forces of repression? Because they are old-fashioned traditionalists, dogmatic and benighted, and sex-ist as well, having obviously neglected to bring a certain other culprit with them? Because we don't choose to observe our own laws against such things as adultery, having come to consider them vestiges of a primitive moral system that we have given up, just as we have given up slavery? Do we think them devious, because we are on the side of Jesus, and we presume that they are not? And, most important of all, do we try to answer such questions by listening to our feelings, or by considering the evidence?

The only evidence we have is in the story, and there is no hint in it that Jesus makes any such judgment of the men who ask him what they ought to do. Nonchalantly, almost as though shrugging, he seems to say, Fine, go ahead. I do know the Law as well as you do. But since you are men who say that you want to know what is right, just be sure that he who throws that first stone is one who knows that *he* is in the right, and that there is no wrongness in him. I, being pedantic, and thus cagey, by profession, talk about wrongness, but he said it right out—without sin.

The religionists of our time would produce so many candidates who would fight for the privilege of throwing that first stone that they would have to raffle it off, thus, as a happy side-effect of righteousness, raising a substantial amount of money for the doing of God's work. But those supposed vigilantes, those rigid dogmatists, those vindictive and self-righteous taunters of a good man, did no such thing. They thought about it, and they dropped their stones, and they went away.

But that isn't exactly true. It is only a "manner of speaking," and manners of speaking, of which there are more than we can count, have a way of deluding the mind. I said that "they" thought about it, but, of course, they didn't. He did. That one right there. And he did too. The man to the left. And that one. And that one. They did not form a committee. They did not hold a meeting. They did not discuss it, considering options and calling for testimony as to opposing points of view, hoping to discover some compromise more or less satisfactory to all parties concerned.

Each one, all alone, considered himself, and nothing but himself. In an act that has come to be thought of as selfish, each one looked into his own goodness without any consideration for the goodness of others, or for their badness either. Each one "minded" his own business, which is to say that each one put his mind to work on himself, seeking his own betterment. And each one found it, and became better.

In this vexatious life, it is not at all uncommon to meet people who call themselves "educators." They swarm. There seem to be millions and millions of them, so many, in fact, that it is nothing short of astonishing that there is anyone left uneducated on the face of Earth. If there were that many orthodontists, you would have to make your way deep into the jungles of Mindanao to find buck teeth. The next time you meet a person who calls himself an educator, ask him this: So, whom have you educated lately? Make sure he gives you their names and addresses.

If you had asked that question of Jesus, as the stone-carriers went their ways, he could have answered, although he probably wouldn't have. He would rather have seen *you* as the smart-alec taunter, and would have found the "right little thing" to say that would cause in you what he had caused in the departing men. If I knew what right little thing he would have said, I would tell you, but I don't. I am not an educator.

But I do know that those men went away educated, "led out" of some captivity, and thinking. And I do know that what Jesus did that day is True Teaching, not asserting, not arguing, not convincing, not demonstrating, not cajoling or threatening, not role-modeling or relating. Just plain teaching. He provided those men with what I have come to think of as an "occasion of education," an irresistible impulse to thoughtfulness, and probably the very sort of thing suggested by the poet who said that "the words of the wise are as goads." They get you moving. And that suggests another question that you might want to put to an educator: When do you educate?

You may have recognized the book that I quoted earlier, the one in which we are given credit for having forsworn cannibalism. About that argument, I can find nothing good to say, but the title of that book is a splendid example of the occasion of education. It is called *Missile Envy*. In that, the author has found one of those right little things to say. It enforces a thought-provoking image—ostensibly grown men, beribboned and bedecked, panting after the bigger and better, fearful lest others have bigger and better. It applies equally as well to missiles as to spears, or even stones, for that title, quite unlike the silly arguments of the passage quoted, points through and beyond particulars to a universal principle by which we see some dark connection between war and lubriciousness, some prurient quality in violence, and by which we are also led to examination of ourselves and our own aggressions and desires for revenge, suddenly and newly revealed as nasty, childish, and shameful. If we could all be impelled to drop our stones, it would be not by the force of the book's argument, but by its title. But that would also require, of course, that we think about it, and about ourselves.

If it is education that is brought about in the would-be stone-throwers, and that might be brought about in us even by just the right little thing, education must have some attributes that we don't ordinarily grant it. For one thing, it is not a " rank," like citizenship or captaincy. It is an inward event, like joy or surprise. It would seem more correct to say, education has sometimes happened to me, than, I am educated. That would also reflect the fact that education is usually temporary, and who is brought to it just now, and in this context, may fall out of it tomorrow, or forget all about it when his belly growls. Thus it can be, for instance, that a highly trained and skillful expert can also be foolish, and utterly uneducated.

And, by token of those same attributes, it seems reasonable to understand education as a possible habit, or propensity, at least, maybe a leaning, an inclination of the mind to notice what the world surely provides—unintended occasions of education. To such a habit, there would have to be added, of course, the habit of looking, of paying attention, and that in itself might well be included in an understanding of education.

Of all the attributes of such a condition, however, there is one that easily escapes our notice, and that will not easily win approval. The condition of the men who chose not to throw their stones was entirely inward, personal and private. What each had come to know, however briefly and incompletely, was himself. And the act by which he had come to that knowledge was done by himself, and could not have been done by another for him. The place where that deed was done is a place where only the self can go—the private, contemplative life of the solitary mind. The fact that it is perfectly possible for human beings to live out life without ever going to that inner place, and *not* the fact that human beings have different mental endowments, is the single greatest impediment to a true education. To that impediment we add another when we disapprove, as socially irresponsible, those who turn inward rather than outward.

Education is neither a social virtue nor a particularly sociable one. In the case of the men in the story, in fact, it brought them to an act that has to be called, changing whatever particulars might need changing, antisocial. They have rejected what their society recognizes not only as a social obligation but as an absolute requirement of religious belief, thus making themselves heretics as well as criminals. They have walked away not only from the criminal, of whose guilt there is no question, but from the Law. They have taken it unto themselves to decide what is right and what is wrong, completely disregarding the opinion of others and the supposed needs of a civilized order. So what are they? Are they heroes or rogues, autonomous men, however briefly, or anarchists?

The question can be put another way: As they disappear from our sight, are they better men or worse? Have they reached some power that they lacked, and given themselves to its use, thus making themselves better men? And is that power not a power of the mind, rather than the power of some other imaginable faculty?

I think those questions might be a bit misleading. They do imply that men who were formerly "bad" became "good" through the use of their minds, but if education and rationality really have the force that I think to find in them, the case is not quite that simple. If education is what makes us "able to be good," as I have said earlier, the change in the stone-carriers must be seen not as a passage from bad to good, but as a growth into the ability to be good. They do not come on the scene as bad men, but only as men who don't know, not as wicked, but as ignorant. Jesus doesn't make them good; they have to do that for themselves. He makes them able.

What was it, then, that had made them *unable*? The power that they discover in the story is surely wonderful, but it is neither miraculous nor unusual. It is a power that we all nod at, when we hear of it, for we all have it, and even use it once in a while, although often under duress. Self-knowledge may be good to have, but whenever I get a flash of it, I find myself hoping that no one else knows what I have just come to know. But we do recognize it for what it is, and recognize it as essentially human, one of the things that makes us different. Surely, those men could have found self-knowledge all by themselves? Why hadn't they? Why did they have to come to Jesus at all?

There is an annoying answer to that question. It has to be something like what we call "faith," a belief, or a collection of beliefs, simply accepted as true and either left unexamined, or of such a nature as to permit no examination, which is to say, made up of worthless statements. Faith is not only religious; it is also social and traditional. The men who came with stones were what we would call "adjusted" to the world of ideas and understandings in which they lived. They were normal. While it turned out that they lacked some very important knowledge, they were not short of information. Far from it, they knew the very letter of the law. Nor were they in any doubt as to the spirit of the law. I can not help thinking of some character in a novel of William Dean Howells who says that it is, of course, possible to be a Christian and still be a good man, but that it is much harder that way. It does seem that it is because of their sincere religiousness, which purrs in the belly, that the would-be stone-throwers have not been able to be good. That seems a bit shocking, but not really any more shocking than a secular equivalent —that it is because of another purr, their public-spirited and dutiful citizenship, that they can not be good.

Although many of us seem to have misunderstood, or even deliberately misconstrued, the nature of education for a very long time, that nature is still recognized in some corner of almost every mind. Our folklore to this day includes the suspicion that education is disruptive, threatening, and all too likely to drive out traditional ideas, values, and beliefs, all of which are granted writs of righteousness by virtue not only of their longevity but equally of their general acceptance. Education is thought the root and also the nourishment of skepticism, the disorder that separates the child from the parent, and even the seed of revolution, which will cancel the very writs of righteousness as though they had never been legitimate. And it is all true.

So how are the stone-carriers different from any other pack of vigilantes? The answer is easy: They have judged *only* themselves, and only upon themselves have they passed sentence. Considering that, I find an extraordinary and unexpected (and also quite unintended) power in the question of the rebukers—What would happen if everyone were to do as you have done? What indeed? I do not know, but it is certainly a tantalizing thought.

Whatever those consequences might be, however, I suspect that we do not have to worry about them very much. The voice of the world is very loud, and easily drowns out the small voice that is in a single person, who is, in any case, *only* a person, and not humanity, which is thought so much more significant. And the belly purrs when we heed the voice of the world, doing our duty and playing our parts in the great scheme of what everybody knows to be right, at least more or less. What the accusers came to notice and consider, when a true teacher told them the right little thing, was that their bellies *were* purring. And the question that they asked of themselves was whether their bellies *should* be purring. Because they *felt* right, doing both their civic and religious duties, did that mean that they *were* right? In each case, each man must have said something like this: As to whether the deed I contemplate is in itself good, which question seems strangely to imply the possibility of a deed with a doer, I am not going to judge. As to whether *I* am good, and should do this deed, I can and will judge. And I'm not, and I shouldn't, and I won't.

As they went away, however, I think that their bellies were not purring. I have had moments of self-knowledge that certainly made me better, but never one that made me *feel* better. So much for the sweetness of Reason.

Now let's try a little experiment in thinking, some consideration of what "we" will have to do if we want to give up war. Giving up war is not entirely unlike the truly extraordinary achievement of the men who came to throw stones. If they did it, why can't we?

But we, of course, are really a tremendous group of "I's." If we are to give up war, then I must be included, and that is all the more necessary if I want to go around and urge others to give up war. My best arguments would fall flat if it could be seen that I was willing to wage war in order to make other people give it up.

The heart of war, the principle by which it lives, is, of course, coercion. It is, in *person*, the desire that is expressed as policy in *humanity*, for those aims that we call "political" rather than personal are still desires that arise in the only place where desires can arise, in persons. When the persons who desire ethnic purity, for instance, are especially influential, and their followers thus numerous, we come to imagine that it is something "bigger" than a merely personal desire, but that bigness is an illusion created by numbers.

Whatever the particular cause of this or that war, its aim is to enforce something on others. If I don't ordinarily use tanks and artillery to coerce others, but only those weapons at my disposal, the coercion is not mitigated into something less than coercion. And the weapons at my disposal are, for my purposes against you, say, just as effective as tanks and artillery. I can wheedle and cajole, I can storm or sulk, I can turn very clever indeed, and turn a fine phrase once in a while. And you may have some of those powers, too, and use them, if only to coerce me into abandoning my attempt to coerce you, for which, we should not forget, many will applaud you as a virtuous fighter against aggression, thus using one of the most telling arguments in favor of war.

Ah but, you may say, that is not truly war. Hostility, aggression, conflict, maybe, but not war. What then, I'll ask, is the essential that I have missed, the thing that makes one aggression or conflict war, and another not war? Violence, you may well answer, and quickly (I suspect) modify that into "physical violence." That too, you will modify, when we have to distinguish between football and such work as that of the police on the one hand, and what you want to mean by war on the other. You will have to move on to lethal and widespread violence against innocent and unconsenting persons, to say nothing of the general destruction of property and even some large portions of the face of the Earth. Thus, however, you will find yourself defining war in such an elaborate and detailed fashion that many of history's most famous and consequential struggles will no longer deserve the name, and the supposed "wars" of prehistoric savages over mates and hunting grounds will have to be seen as nothing more than trivial squabbles.

As soon as we start measuring ideas like war by numbers or size, we give up hope of understanding them. If there is one slave, there is slavery. It takes only one persistent cannibal to ensure the continuation of cannibalism. Is there some number of warriors, or tanks, in whose lack war ceases to be war? When Arthur and Mordred are the last combatants on the field, has war given way to a family spat, or would it be better designated as a case of dueling?

And we also give up hope of understanding them when we try to define our ideas by their supposed consequences. War is that which causes death, and deaths beyond counting? What doesn't? Everyone living will die, and every building now standing will fall down, and all that we know will pass away. War is that which brings misery and deprivation to millions? Do not millions live in misery and deprivation due to many things other than war? What is *the* difference between war and plague, between war and the mere passage of time that will bring an end to everything that is?

What else can it be but something in the heart, the intention to coerce, and the willing acceptance of coercion as a way of bringing about some result presumed good? No one ever fomented a war, or signed up to fight it, for what he knew to be evil purposes. Only in comic books. If the root of war is our belief that coercion is sometimes necessary and justifiable, coupled with the lessons of experience by which we know that coercion often succeeds very well indeed, and if the "good" remains among us a matter of one opinion as against another, one interest against another, one unverifiable belief against another, then it is very unlikely that "we" can give up war.

But *you* could give up war. And so could I. And that would mean that we would reject the use of coercion under any circumstances whatsoever, and, accordingly, abandon all claims to any "rightness" that can not be incontrovertibly demonstrated, like the square of the hypotenuse, to others. It would mean also that we restrict ourselves to committing only those deeds that pertain to a person, and refraining from those deeds that can pertain only to humanity.

I don't think that would be a bad condition, but some are sure to say of it that it is not to the point. What good will it do, many would ask, if I give up war, and all those other people don't? That won't bring an end to war. Which is to say, of course, *I* am not the cause of war. It's all those *other* people, whoever they might be, the ones who say that they are against war, but obviously don't mean it.

I wouldn't know what to say to that, of course, but I would have a very interesting question for you: What would become of us all, what would happen to civilization as we know it, if everyone did what you have decided that it would be useless to do?

FIVE

The
GIFT
of
FIRE

I WENT TO TALK TO THE MEN-
sans. The members of Mensa are the smartest people in America, and I was intimidated. I was afraid that they might catch me in a circular argument or a lexigraphical fallacy. I was afraid that they would rise up, right in the middle of the pathetic little lecture I had thought up for them, and demolish my silly little premises, and then go, not storming, but laughing, from the room, to hold high converse among themselves, not even offering me any coffee and doughnuts.

The speech was meant to be the opener of a small convention, and scheduled to take place right after breakfast. I got there early, and was sent to join the Mensans in a room on the fourth floor, in an upper room, where they were standing around having coffee and doughnuts. I was relieved of at least one of my fears. But they were all watching television, and no one said anything to me. I stood around for a while and went back downstairs, where the brisk young woman who had sent me upstairs told me that I would have to understand that Mensans never did anything on schedule, and that I would have to wait till they came down, Soon, maybe.

I sat in the lobby and read some of the Mensan handouts that I found on the floor near the sofa. One of them was a sample test. To become a Mensan, you have to get high grades on some tests, and what I was reading was a kind of prep for those tests. It had some very interesting questions. One of them asked which diagram of a group of six would be generated by taking diagram C and subjecting it to whatever operations had transformed diagram A into diagram B. Or maybe it was the other way around. There was a very good train question, whose details I can't recall, but it had all the classical attributes of train questions—train A and train B leaving at different times from points C and D, moving at rates E and F, and meeting, at last, at the mysterious point X, where ships also, I suppose, pass in the night. It really took me back. But the question I liked best of all went something like this:

> Bob and Carol and Alice and Ted all took the Mensa test. Bob scored higher than Alice, who scored ten points lower than Ted. Ted's score added to Carol's score and then divided by the difference between Bob's score and Alice's score was either twenty points more or twelve points less than the average of all four scores. Which of the four made it into Mensa?

Well, I may have forgotten some of the less important details. But it was a great question.

I had planned to start my talk to the Mensans with some mention of Prometheus, and to quote a little from Aeschylus. It was the passage in which Prometheus, about to be chained down for quite a long time, makes a little recitation of the things he has done for humanity, and in which he does not mention at all what we usually think of—the gift of fire. He speaks instead of such powers as those of language and number, and, most important of all, the mind's grasp of itself, in Locke's words. It is the ability not only to think, but to think about thinking. Before humanity had that, Prometheus says, humans lived a random and aimless life, "all blindly floundering on from day to day." I knew that the Mensans were people interested in their minds, as people should be, and I thought that I might encourage them in that interest, and, at the same time, give due praise to the great minds of the past who understood long ago that the mind's grasp of itself is what alone makes possible the examined life, and thus the good life.

So I imagined myself in conversation with Prometheus, who had come back to find out what we mortals had managed to do with the astounding powers that he had given to us alone of all creatures.

How fortunate I am to run into you, he began, for I see by

your rumpled clothing and your knitted brow that you must be in the mind business.

I'm honored to meet you, Sir, I replied, and I will confess that I am in the mind business, for I do no heavy lifting. Would you care to have some coffee and doughnuts with the Mensans?

Not just now, thank you. I have come, I must admit, not for social reasons, but on business. Long, long ago I gave you all the power of the mind's grasp of itself, the fire by which you may burn and glow like no other mortal creature. That got me into a lot of trouble at first, of course, but since my release I've had long, long ages of time in which to wonder whether or not I had done the right thing. I have grown so curious, in fact, that I have now undertaken, as you see, a journey whose enormousness you can not imagine, and only for the purpose of finding out to what good uses you have put my gift.

Aha, I said, you have come not only to the right man, but to the right place, and also at the right time. There must be something to that Divine Guidance business. As it happens, I hold here in my hand the answer that you seek.

What have we done, you ask. Just listen to this. Imagine a train leaving point A and moving toward point B at the rate of C. Imagine now another train moving from B to A at rate D, having set forth on its journey E minutes after the departure of the first train. Would you believe it if I told you that we—well, some of us—are able to figure out where and when those trains will meet? So how's that for mind business?

He looks at me steadily for a moment. He clears his throat. I begin to feel that I have not yet fully stated our case. I rush into the silence with six diagrams.

And look at this, just look at this. You see these diagrams? Now this little one over here was made by doing something or other, maybe a little twisting or turning this way or that, to this other little diagram. Now, and this is the beauty part, one of these six diagrams down here got to be the way it is because the very same things, the twisting and turning stuff, you know, were done to *this* little diagram. Pretty neat, eh? Now suppose I were to tell you that we—well, some of us—by the power of *the mind alone,* can say exactly which of these little...

At this point, Prometheus silently rises and begins to walk off. I get the impression, probably through Divine Guidance, that he is going to go back and chain himself to the rock for another long sentence.

Wait, wait, I call after him, now heading through the door and out into the street. Let me tell you about Bob and Carol and Alice and Ted! They all took this test, you see, and... and...

But Prometheus is gone. I begin to wonder whether the nature of his gift is such that he can take it back. I begin to suspect that he *has* taken it back. My mind is losing the grasp of itself. All I can think of is Bob and Alice and Carol and Ted drawing little diagrams while traveling on a train from point A to point B at the rate of C.

What should we mean by "intelligence"? I think it is important to ask the question in just that way—What *should* we mean? This seems to me an essential rule of thought, that when we talk about things that do not simply appear to us as a part of the world, we take on a grave responsibility to each other and to ourselves. Such things as intelligence and love and patience are possible only where there is a person. We do not find them lying around so that we can weigh and measure them, so there truly is no such thing as deciding whether love is the "true" kind or some other. We *can*, of course, mean anything we please by such terms, and just as easily mean one thing today and another tomorrow. In the best possible world, we probably would know better than to talk about such things at all, and we probably wouldn't have to. However, if the mind is to take the grasp of itself, and if we are to instruct ourselves in the art of taking that grasp, we must end up talking about things like intelligence. And love. And patience. And whatever else "exists," in some strange way, because persons exist.

Is it by the very same power that we can, in one case, conclude that it is better to suffer an injustice than to do one, and, on the other, discover which of six diagrams was generated by what process? Do we use the same faculty to consider whether patience can and should be cultivated and to tell where the trains will meet?

My questions, I know, seem to imply that we don't use the same power or faculty in all of those cases, but I truly don't know that. Whatever it is by which we do such things, it is not a fish that I can show you so that you might check what I have said about it, and I do not want to pretend that it is a fish, and speak of it as something that we all can see and measure. For when people do pretend that it is a fish, some strange things happen.

Let me rephrase a question just a little bit. Which will be detected by an intelligence test: the ability to make some rationally demonstrable conclusion as to whether suffering injustice is better than inflicting it, or the ability to tell where the trains will meet? Is it possible that we might meet some person who does indeed give himself to consider whether patience is a fixed or a changeable attribute, but can not for the life of him tell you which diagram was made from which? And one more question: How did the makers of the intelligence test come to "know" what intelligence is, that they can devise ways to measure it, and then pronounce its worth in numbers?

In detail, I can not answer. In principle, I can. They made certain choices. They made them, probably, for what they deemed very practical reasons, but with consequences that are not best described as merely practical. They have given the rest of us ideas, of which we may not even be thoughtfully aware, and by which we may, and often do, make choices of our own. We choose, for instance, every bit as much in families as in schools, how to train the minds of children, and which children to subject to which form of training, in accordance with some packaged and delivered ideas about intelligence. On the basis of those decisions, we commit acts, acts that have consequences in the very deepest centers of persons. That is a perilous business.

And that is why I ask: What *should* we mean by intelligence? It is not a question of fact, for there is no fact; it is a moral question. There is "shouldness" in it.

The word "intelligence" comes from two Latin words, *inter* and *legere*, which, put together, suggest the act of one who looks around among different things and makes choices, gathering some and leaving others. That is a portrayal of a mental activity very different from figuring out where the trains meet, but also an act that is a little bit like discovering the right diagram. But only a little bit. The idea of intelligence includes not only the choosing, but the chooser, an agent who chooses to choose. But when you choose the right diagram, you are not truly doing your own choosing. You are walking in someone else's footprints, and the "rightness" of your choice is in having done what someone else has already done.

There is a special case of thinking that is called problem-solving. Solving a problem is not the same thing as understanding a principle. It is, however, the sort of thinking that we have come to accept as the mark of intelligence, and the thinking that some people seem to like a lot. Somebody chose that understanding. Not one somebody, of course, but many somebodies, and I deceive myself and you if I say that "we" have either chosen it or that we have come to adopt it. Certain people did all that. Haphazardly. And now we live by it. We fashion our schools to match it, and measure their "products" by its yardstick. And thus we will win the disapproval of Prometheus and then perhaps even the loss of his gift.

I think I may lead myself into confusion if I accept without thinking Locke's name for the gift of Prometheus—"the mind's grasp of itself." There is no such thing as *the* mind; where there is mind there is *a* mind. It is not *the* mind that my mind might be able to grasp, but only *my* mind. I will not be able to take the grasp of your mind, nor you of mine, and for that we are both properly grateful. Some things are better kept private. When I do set out to take the grasp of my mind, I must find myself walking into unknown, and perhaps very dangerous, territory, where no one has ever gone before. I can find models of that journey, and accounts of other such journeys in other minds, but I can not find *that* journey. I end up doing, therefore, what is absolutely unique to me, and what, should I not do it, can not be done.

But when I solve Mensan problems, that is not the case. There, I will be doing what others have done. But those are, of course, problems that seem fake, somehow. Somebody cooked them up to *be* problems. They are a kind of game, a trivial pursuit. There is something to be learned in such a practice, of course, some habits of consistency and attentiveness, but in those who have learned those habits from earlier problems, the industrious solution of later problems, more of the same, seems a bit childish. The great charm of problem-solving lies in tackling the problems that have not been solved, which is to say, the problems that have never before arisen.

Such problems are almost always related to technology, and their solutions seem wondrous to us not because they come from newly devised powers of the mind, but always because they provide some new thing in the world. In that respect, microwave relay stations and eggbeaters are similar, both wonders. The most important difference between them is that Attila the Hun would have given you Asia Minor for the latter, but nothing at all for the former.

There is a sense in which the unsolved problem, even the problem that has yet to appear to us, is already "solved." You can provide your own easy example of the fact by making up your own train problem, using whatever numbers please you. You don't have to stick to trains. Airplanes or ox carts will do as well. What you now have is a "new" problem, a never-before solved problem. But, of course, its solution does exist. Although you can not make it just now, there is a statement that you will be able to make once you have made the statements that lead to it. That's how any problem is solved, however complicated, and however long.

Problem-solving is a wonderful device, and fun, but it ought to be kept in its place. The best way to do that is through a careful use of language. When I say that I have a problem, my first thought should be to consider as well as I can whether it truly is a problem. As to the meeting of the trains, I have little doubt. When I consider the problem of rearing children sanely and decently, or the problem of making ends meet, I become uneasy. And when it comes to World Peace and the Brotherhood of All Mankind, I am frightened, frightened of what will happen to us if we imagine that such grand hopes are to be realized by the process of problem-solving. In such matters, can the pertinent facts be known? Can anyone know when he has them all? Can they be tested and found as "true" as those given in train problems, or even in the most elaborate and complicated possible versions of train problems?

Where human beings are concerned, can we ever have all the facts? Can we ever *know* that we do, or that we don't? If we imagine that human dilemmas can be unraveled by that sort of thinking that problem-solving represents, are we not likely to run into something more vexing than problems?

That social and moral human "problems" have proved insoluble for the whole history of our species up to now, is not the least bit surprising, and it is exactly by the gift of Prometheus that we can know that. When we consider and question, and come to have some understanding of the process of problem-solving and its necessary attributes, we are *not* solving a problem. We are understanding. A mind is taking some grasp of itself. Because it is a mind, its understanding will be *its* understanding, not *the* understanding, and what it understands, however more or less, will be itself and its work, not *the* mind and *its* work. Not even another mind and its work. As to your mind, I do suspect that mine can make some pretty good guesses, even theories, but they *are* guesses and theories.

Problem-solving is something that we can *also* do by the gift of Prometheus. Understanding is *the* thing that we can do by that gift. The light of problem-solving is like the light of the moon, a reflection of some greater light. And when we single out the skills of problem-solving and give them the name of intelligence, we make a choice between the moon and the sun, and run the danger of putting out our own fires.

There is, in all of those dilemmas and mysteries that arise from the unfathomables of our humanity, a hauntingly familiar quality, as though we were all doing everything again and again. Thus it was, for instance, that Freud could conclude that Sophocles was not just right, but *still* right, perhaps *always* right. And it is to help us understand not the quaint beliefs of primitive and unscientific people, but, quite simply, ourselves—at any time, and in any place.

As fire is given in the myth, fire is given again and again in each of us, as it must once have been given to creatures who by its power became human. Like the species, we have all lived out of an impenetrable antiquity into the now. Every one of us must awaken out of sleep and come into the light of self-mindedness. And when self-mindedness arises, when the mind first comes to consider itself and *knows* that it considers itself, it is in language. It seems that the propensity for language and the propensity for self-mindedness are the same thing, which is, really, not sufficiently distinguished by the word "propensity." "Destiny" seems better. We are the creatures who are destined to think and to know themselves, and that is the gift of Prometheus.

Nobody knows when all that happened, but everybody who knows anything can see that it must have happened. Every single one of us lives again the astonishing and utterly unaccountable history of the coming into this world of the truly human. And we do it, for there is no other way, one by one. It is not humanity that comes into the grasp of the mind. It is a person that comes into the grasp of that person's mind. Information and examples I can take, in that degree to which I am literate, curious, and attentive, from countless other persons, most of them long dead but still speaking to me, but I must discover thoughtfulness for and in myself and come to understand for the first time what I have never understood before and what no one else can understand for me, any more than he might nourish me by his eating or refresh me by his sleep.

Nevertheless, while no one else can nourish me, I will never be nourished by those who are not themselves nourished, never brought into thoughtfulness unless others have gone there before me. This is, I think, a great mystery, and the most powerful suggestion I know that two seemingly contradictory possibilities are both true: that the individual person is the root and dwelling place of all that is truly human, and that society is the root and dwelling place of all that is truly human. Unless, of course, there really was a Prometheus, who started the whole business, out of nothing.

But if there was, he has obviously gone away and left us to what we must call, lacking better knowledge, our own devices. And our own devices are pretty good. As persons, we do make society, and as society, we do make persons. The enterprise of education is entangled in that paradox, and it is the proper business of everybody both to nourish and to be nourished, both to take the grasp of his own mind and to provide for others the power to do the same. It is for that reason that we properly connect the idea of education with the rearing of children. As to which of us are truly the children, we really have no clear idea, but we do know that there are children among us, and that something should be done about them. If we knew exactly what that was, and who the children were, there could be education.

CHILDREN
and
FISH

ABOUT A CENTURY AGO, A
certain Edward Bellamy wrote a visionary novel about the
distant future, about our time, in fact. It was called *Looking
Backward*, and it was the first of all best-sellers in this land. I
find it silly and boring, for most of it is made up of little
lectures on social betterment delivered by a wise mentor
who universally and uncritically approves of everything that
his society is doing. But no matter, for in that book there are
about four pages of inestimable worth. The mentor, who is
called Dr. Leete, explains the principles upon which that society has grounded its understanding of the term education,
and proceeds to enumerate certain "rights" that it has
granted its citizens in regard to education.

The first of them is the right to enjoy life as fully as possible. That means, among other things, the right to have those
powers that provide some access both to the works of the
mind that can delight and illuminate, and to the working of
the mind, which does the same. Dr. Leete would say of us
that leaving people in that condition in which they can neither know nor govern themselves is a violation of their
rights, and an outrage.

If that is the right to *be* educated, the second is the right to
live among *other* educated people, for the former is generally
the root of unhappiness in the lack of the latter. If, between
the minded and the unminded, there is the equivalent of class
struggle, there will be perpetual contempt and animosity on
both sides, leaving the members of neither able to enjoy life
fully.

The third right, and the one that most especially interests
me here, is even more shocking and portentous than the first
two, for it is one of those rights assigned specifically not to
all, but only to a certain group, and thus sounds suspiciously
like a privilege rather than a right. It is the right of children
to be reared by educated parents. It is not an idea that could
ever take hold among us, for it would surely lead to riot and
civic discord, but, since we often mean by "education"

nothing more than some supposedly acceptable indoctrination, it seems also an idea that should not be allowed to take hold among us.

But it is a truly and usefully provocative idea. Can there be a greater misfortune than to be reared by silly and self-indulgent parents, parents who have no inklings either of self-knowledge or self-government? If children of such parents ever reach those powers, will it not be by sheer, and unlikely, luck? We can look around our world and identify them very easily, the children of children. They are in a condition as desperate as that of the children of the House of Atreus. "Doom, like a black wave out of the West, rises over them." In Dr. Leete's scheme of things, they are, while utterly without guilt of their own, a disaster that must inevitably strike us all, depriving us of the first two rights, and making the good life impossible for everyone, and they are themselves incapable of finding that life.

But "incapable" is not the best word. "Incapacitated" would be better. It is not because of what they *are* that they can not hope for self-knowledge and self-government, but because of what has been done to them. And because of what has *not* been done in their presence. Education is not something that one person does to another. Like the stone-carriers, we have to do it in ourselves, one by one. Their teacher did not wait to measure their intelligence quotients or cognitive modalities, or devise some test of their listening skills; he simply did what was right. He did not excuse himself from the task of teaching them on the ground of their "learning disabilities." If we could send Jesus a new and utterly unteachable pack of stone-carriers, it could only be because we had incapacitated in them the native ability to seek the good. To do that—can it really be done?—would be simply to make of a human being something less than human.

We give no noticeable thought as to how we might, deliberately and by underlying principle rather than pragmatic detail, take the greatest possible care to *avoid* making something less than human of human beings. And if we were to make that consideration into a goal of schooling, we would engender nothing but hosts of people who want to form a committee that will draw up the guidelines for a tentative plan of action to be submitted for approval to a commission that will go to work on the assignment of research grants to institutes that will devise timetables and flowcharts to facilitate the establishment of an agency with an agenda for the drafting of recommended legislation to be presented to an appropriate committee. That may not help.

I, however, *can* help, provided that I think not of going out to make the world a better place, but only of going *in* to make the world a better place. Out there, I have little chance, I think. A number of others have failed. Many of them were more skillful and influential than I. Like the stone-carriers, I am a legal grown-up, and a frequent child. *That* is the child that I am given, before all others, to rear. In those terms it is possible to reach a fairly practical, everyday understanding of what Socrates meant by the examined life; it is nothing but the rearing of the child that I am, and the deliberate doing, in his presence, of the right thing. Perhaps someday I will become able to make the world a better place, but that can hardly be expected in one who can not rear wisely that one who is most utterly and completely his own child.

Consider, therefore, the rearing of children. Consider it even if you imagine that you do not have any children. Do not bother to try to count the various current theories as to how this is best done, and don't even think of all the old theories that we now, if only for a while, find bunk. In fact, don't even think of "the rearing of children." There is no such thing. "Children" can not be reared. To do some rearing, you need a child. Everyone has at least one. Imagine that you are that parent, and that you intend to rear that child.

What do you want her to be like? I suspect that you want her to be good and to be happy. I suspect also that you want her to be successful, too, and not only because she might then be able to support you in your old age, but because success is obviously better than failure, and more likely to provide happiness. Thus, you will want her to be industrious, but not obsessed with work, and effective. You might also want her to be someone who will someday be able to rear her own child as wisely as you reared her.

All of those aims at least *sound* realistic. They seem to be things that you can do something about. Some other possible aims, however, are not realistic. While you would surely like her to be smart and pretty, she may be neither of those things. She may not even be tall and thin. You can, of course, and almost certainly will, have her teeth straightened and keep her clean, but that is about as far as you can go in making changes in what might be called a certain and fixed portion of the endowment with which she came into this world. It will be useful to you, in your task of wise child-rearing, to be mindful of what can be brought about and what can't. Let us call, for convenience, that which can not be changed by the name of Necessity. Whatever it is, it is. The best we can do is to hope that there isn't too much of it, and that what there is of it does not preclude such things as goodness and happiness, or even whatever we mean by success.

So we consider what you *can* do. Let's start with seeing to it that she is good. Of what does that quality consist? How does one be good? Are certain deeds good and others bad by nature? Are we good or bad by temperament or genetic endowment? Are good and bad relative conditions, like rich and poor, providing some broad middle ground of the mostly OK? Don't answer those questions. Ask this one first: Have they already been answered?

Of course. A million times, but not in a million ways. The answers to such questions come in just a few standard brands, but they all have certain things in common. The answerers have traditionally imagined that goodness itself comes in at least two standard brands. It is out of one sort of goodness that a child refrains from throwing grapefruit around in the supermarket, and out of another that she habitually tells the truth. You will, I am sure, want her to have as much as possible of each, but I am just as sure that you will prize the latter somewhat more than the former. Naturally. But why do I suppose that preference "natural"? Is it really?

For just a while, forget the little girl. She will wait. Ask yourself that question again. Is it indeed natural that the one sort of goodness is more to be prized than the other? That question would not appear on an intelligence test, and its answer, if it has one, would not be like the solution of a problem, not a "correctness" like the meeting place of the trains. It would lack the quality of public verifiability, which is surely an essential attribute of solutions. That is actually good news, not bad, for even if you haven't mastered the trick of choosing the right diagram, even if you don't give a hoot as to the destinies of Bob and Alice and Carol and Ted, you are nevertheless the one and only power that we know of in the universe that can give thought to its own thought, a mind with the gift of fire. So stop reading for a few minutes and answer the question: Is it natural to prefer that goodness which impels truthfulness to that which impels acceptable behavior?

I presume that you have made your answer. (Such answers, unlike the solutions of problems, seem best described as "made" rather than discovered.) Your answer is a good one. I am perfectly safe in saying that. Any answer to such a question is better than no answer; and one who is willing to rest content with no answer at all, or without even asking the question, shouldn't be allowed near children anyway. Who wants a child to be "good" ought to have *some* idea what he means by that, and some idea as to how to *have* some idea. Children reared out of thoughtlessness are in danger.

My answer went something like this: I remembered Socrates talking about the difference between *being* good and *seeming* good. It is obviously possible that the outward appearance of goodness is a sign of inward goodness, but it is just as possible that it is not. As to which is which, experience is a remarkably poor teacher. So I imagined some rearer of a child who actually did prefer the goodness of social acceptability to the inner goodness of truthfulness, who said, in effect, I care not at all what she is like inwardly, but only what the world imagines that she must be like inwardly. I will see to it that she behaves impeccably both in supermarkets and salons, a practice which, it must be admitted, is not always possible to those who are truthful by habit and intent. From that, I went to wondering what I might call such a would-be rearer of children, asking also whether I would want to give him charge of one of mine. I decided against it. I went further, and found in him something that I had to call perversity, a twist, a disorder that seemed to make of him something not entirely human, and thus, unnatural. So I concluded, roughly but readily, that if it is unnatural to prefer the goodness of social acceptability to the goodness of truthfulness, then the contrary condition might well be deemed "natural." My answer raises, I know, swarms of other questions, but it is an answer, and I made it. If my answer has brought about some revisions in your answer— good. If it brings about, now that I can look at it, some revisions in itself, good. If I could know yours, I would surely be able to improve mine, and that would be good. And, so far at least, we have not had to consult Dr. Spock. Also good.

But what, exactly, do we know? We know this: That wanting a child to be good is not enough to bring her to that condition, and that we had better know what we mean by "good." We even have to know which good is the better, and, if there seem to be many sorts of good, which is the best—for which most parents cross their fingers and hope.

Consider the finger-crossers, hoping for the best. It can be out of only one condition that they do that, the very condition out of which we have just come, a tiny step or two—ignorance. It is because they don't know what the best is that they have to hope for it, and can find no way to pursue it. And they face the sad certainty that, should the best in fact come to pass, they wouldn't be able to recognize it. They would be in like predicament as to the worst. We do not know what the best is either, but we do know that one "goodness" may be better than another goodness. That is something. And we know also that we are able to discover whether one goodness is better than another. And that is a big something.

Because of what you know, you are going to have some difficulties in the rearing of that child, difficulties perhaps never dreamed of by those who don't know what you know. It is simply a fact that the two goodnesses at issue do, and not infrequently, collide with each other in a terrible crash. Which to follow, and when? How to learn that delicate art? And how—an even more difficult question—how to teach it to a child in whom there is yet no power of discourse, no familiarity with the abstract or with principle, no mind's grasp of itself?

When Socrates made his preposterous defense to the jury that was going to convict him no matter what he said, he warned the jurors that, should they make the mistake of setting him free, he intended to embark at once on a career of recidivism. I will surely commit, every day, he said, the crime of which I am accused, which is nothing other than talking about goodness. We imagine, because Socrates has been rehabilitated by most of Western thought, that the jurors who weren't vindictive must have been simply confused, and supposed that what Socrates called "talking about goodness" was really something else. How, after all, could anyone who had come to, and rested in, his senses object to talking about goodness?

But I suspect that those jurors who weren't out for revenge had, nevertheless, some pretty strong reasons for finding that practice dangerous to the health of the body politic. I suspect also that some of them—how lucky we are that they are gone—might find the same of your considerations as to which sort of goodness is the better, and why. What ordinarily masquerades as "talking about goodness" is really nothing more than the recitation of precepts, perhaps with footnotes. Which precepts are recited will depend on that party of the reciter, who is, more often than not, an "expert" in goodness. Usually with a license. From his party.

Our trouble in noticing this comes from the preposition. When we talk "about" fish, and keep strictly to the subject, not talking at all about ourselves and how *we* feel about fish, we are stuck with a reality that has nothing to do with us. Fish are fish. About fish, we can make demonstrably true or false statements. No matter what we say, the fish remain what they are. When Socrates described his crime as talking about goodness, he meant a different kind of "about." It is an about not of description but of discovery, not of prescription but of predication, whose limits are not dictated by a reality that has nothing to do with us, but by a reality that has *everything* to do with us, and is what it is only because and when we make it. In fish there is no good or bad, no fair or foul, no right or wrong. In us, the case is otherwise.

Those who talk about goodness, therefore, are indeed something of a danger to the peace and health of the body politic. They are asking what goodness is, in spite of having been told a thousand times, and whether they might discover and understand it for themselves, and in their own minds, in spite of the popular belief of every body politic in our time that goodness is not the proper business of the intellect, but of feelings and beliefs, and, of course, the proper business of a few highly trained specialists.

There is, in fact, some threat to the tranquility of society in talking about anything *except* fish. As long as we stick to fish, or to any of countless equivalents in the world as provided to us, we are very unlikely to fall out with one another and come to blows. But the world as provided to us is not *the* world, for there is also the mind-made world, which is not subject to the test of hard experience that can force us to agree as to fish. We can't even come to agreement, and probably shouldn't, as to how far one's "family" extends, or as to the meaning and purpose of banking, to say nothing of intelligence—or goodness. That is good, for it permits us to *make* such conceptions, and to remake them. But it also permits us to make and remake them wisely or foolishly, and to be either blessed or stuck with them.

Goodness is not fish. In thinking how to rear a child, therefore, your talking about goodness is truly a way of considering whether you are blessed or burdened with the ideas about goodness that you happen to hold, for whatever reasons. If we suppose, for instance, that intelligence is measurable by the skill of problem-solving, are we blessed or burdened with that idea? If intelligence were a thing that exists on its own, like a fish, there would be no point in asking such a question. But it isn't. We do not have to settle for it. We make it, and live with what we make.

Children, also, are not fish. There are many ways to define children, and the silliest possible one is the one that we usually use. Age. But, in asking yourself how to talk about goodness with the little girl you hope to rear wisely, and realizing that she has not yet found the grasp of her own mind, you have already come up with a far better definition. To understand that children are those under the age of eighteen is an idea that we are stuck with. We do need some such arrangement for the sake of ordering affairs in the body politic. But *you* need not be stuck with it. If you should prefer to understand that children are those human beings who have not yet found the grasp of their own minds, then the task you have given yourself, that task of rearing a child wisely and well, is suddenly transformed from indoctrination to education, in its truest sense, and made not only possible but even likely—provided, to be sure, one little prerequisite, which is that *you* are not a child, that you have come into the grasp of your mind.

Bad news, eh? I know just how you feel.

Understanding what I *do* think, and *why* I think it, and whether I *should* think it, is, at best, an occasional and fleeting condition. I would be delighted beyond describing, but utterly astonished as well, to meet anyone who was always secure in such understandings. I have no such hope. But if my mind, like any operating mind, can reach that condition once in a while, why is it that it so often doesn't?

For an answer to that question, and for another valuable hint about the rearing of children, we can go to Aristotle. He provides an intriguing definition of "children," a simple little idea whose implications are tremendous. Children, he said, are those who are completely governed by their appetites. He didn't mean to insult them, as mere brute creatures. He meant only to name their *nature*. It is *by nature* that children are whatever it is that they are. And it is equally by nature that they become, or can become something other than what they were.

He is, if he is doing any judging at all, excusing children by saying that they are governed by their appetites. If that is so, then we can not say of children that they are "bad." To be bad requires an act of the will, a knowing choice, and, stangely enough, *self-government*. Children can't govern themselves. Not yet. By the same token, however, we can not say of them that they are "good." To be good is not simply to refrain from being bad. It is an act, a willed and chosen act. I suppose, therefore, that he would not have

found you or me either good or bad because of *the act* that
we commit, but because of the *choosing* that informs it. If I
do refrain from throwing grapefruit in the supermarket, it
does not prove me good simply because I don't happen to
want to.

The rearing of children thus must begin at home. I mean
really at home. In me. In anyone. In those times when I am
governed by my appetites, I am the child who needs rearing.
I am not able to talk about goodness, for my appetites have
already done the talking, and told me that goodness is getting what I want.

Imagine what sort of a teacher I must be in that condition.
If it is my appetite for admiration and self-esteem that has
seized me, an appetite which we are strangely encouraged to
arouse in each other, how likely am I to remember, as a
teacher should always remember, that I am standing between my students and the light? I am not that light, and it is
my job to open my students' eyes to the light, not to the
flash of my own cleverness. But which will I do? Would you
want me, in that state, to rear your child?

Are we any less mindless if we depend on others to tell us
what is good? How have those tellers escaped the regular
recurrence of childhood that strikes you and me? I wish they
would tell us not only what is good, but how they came to
know that. If they have learned to take so firmly the grasp of
their own minds that they can always recognize and disarm
the insidious and amiable promptings of appetite, which
they must have done to become experts on the good, I wish
they would just give us the secret of that power, so that we
too may become experts on the good. Then we could understand *in principle* the difference between the better and the
worse, and those who now counsel us so assiduously would
be spared the trouble of rating as good or bad all of the
countless particulars of human action.

And while we are asking such questions of those who
would counsel us, let us ask them as well of ourselves, who

are also setting out as counselors of others, as those who would rear this little girl to be good and happy.

Many of those who counsel us as to goodness will say that it is not by the power of Reason that goodness can be understood. They do not agree, however, as to what power it is by which we can understand goodness. Some will say "character," in some rough sense of the word, believing that some people are just inclined that way, and others less so, some few, in fact, are remarkably disinclined to goodness. Some will say that it is by example, a sort of subliminal experience, that we learn to be good or to be bad. Some will even say that it is out of the frustration of appetite that we do bad, and out of its satisfaction that we can afford to be good. Many will say that goodness is known by the conscience, an invisible table of laws that can somehow be generated in the mind, thus disputing themselves if they also say, as they tend to, that it is not by the mind that we can know the good. And many more will say that we can know the good by precept, by hearing and believing some Truth that is provided for us, and not by some power of our own, but by some power that is outside of us. And there are lots and lots of people who say all of those things, at one time or another, and lots more who don't say anything at all. They just live.

I do not know which of them is right, or if any one of them is right. But I keep thinking of the square of the hypotenuse, and a strange kind of truth that can be known by Reason, and only by Reason. Example and experience will never show it. No instinct or hunch or deep feeling, however sincere, will lead me to believe it. No authority, no voice of this world or any other, however sonorous, will convince me by force. But when my reason has walked the path, which is the proof of it, I have pure knowledge that carries its own license, and not the badge of any interest. It may be that goodness can not be known by Reason, but I will be ready to accept that only after I have done all that Reason permits and found it wanting.

I won't be able to do that until I manage to grow up. Child-rearing is not some special part of life, set aside for some temporary purpose and put aside at a certain age. It is the principal business of life, the search for the condition that is naturally promised for us by the fact of our life. And we must do it in ourselves, one by one.

SEVEN

The
PERILS
of
PETRONILLA

HERE IS AN ENTERTAINING
and instructive story about the rearing of children, those in
us as well as those out there, and about goodness and happiness, and how they can be known.

Saint Peter, the tale tells, had an only and much beloved
daughter named Petronilla. Peter knew all too well the
wicked ways of the world, and the terrible temptations it
had to offer, especially to attractive young girls. He wanted,
as we all do, to keep his daughter safe, lest she fall into any
badness, and thus, I suppose, also to keep her happy, for
badness is a notorious provider of unhappiness.

He was a man of considerable and very unusual powers,
so he brought upon the girl a deep slumber, almost like that
of death itself. And so she slept her young years away, safe
from the world and its wickedness. Peter's friends, however,
knew only that the girl was always unconscious, like one
deathly ill.

One day, when some of them came to visit and chat with
the great man, one of them said:

Peter, we find one thing hard to understand. We have seen
you work wonders with the sick and even those at the very
door of death. How is it then, that you seem to be able to do
nothing for your own child, your lovely daughter, who lies
as one dead in the next room, and has so lain for years?

Ah, my friends, said Peter, you misunderstand. Petronilla
is not sick at all. She sleeps, and I have provided her the safe
haven of that sleep. Thus she will escape that which so
threatens and often undoes even the best of mortals, the cor-
rupting influence of this world and its ways. She is far from
sick; she is well in virtue, and sleeps exactly as I want her to
sleep. Here, let me show you that what I say is true.

And he called the girl to awaken. And she awoke. Come,
said her father, and meet my friends. Bring them food and
drink, that we may be joyful together. And she brought
them food and drink, and Saint Peter's friends found the girl
just as he had said, pure and good and gracious in every way,

and uncorrupted by the world. And when she had done all that was asked of her, her father sent her back to bed. Sleep now, Petronilla, he said. And she slept.

That's one of my favorite stories. It provokes endless thought, all of it fruitful, but unfortunately a bit facetious. We don't educate children that way anymore, but we have gone to the opposite and equally ludicrous extreme. We don't let them get any sleep at all. Even as tiny tykes, they are led to worry about any and every great social issue from abortion to nuclear war, and cajoled into believing that they have done something about such matters once they have expressed themselves. Their geography books require them to speculate as to what they would do to put an end to poverty in South America, and their civics books call on them to imagine a solution to the problem of toxic waste which requires nothing more than the miraculous appearance of some currently unknown technology. They are thus led to believe first of all that great human mysteries can be boiled down into something very much like a train problem, and thereafter that anyone at all, whatever the depth of his ignorance, can make the world a better place by relating well to others and muddling through. The condition of children thus deluded is, of course, very different from that of Petronilla, but it isn't any better.

The story of Petronilla, obviously apocryphal but once popular among the faithful, is a clue to a great and influential event of our history that goes unmentioned in our texts. When, exactly, it befell us all, I don't know, but by simple logic I do know that it must have happened.

There was a time, and we can easily see it in the five or six centuries that run roughly from the time of Socrates to the time of Epictetus, when the idea of education was very simple, and the supposed consequences of education, tremendous. With us, it is the other way around. The process of education is tremendously complicated and technical, filled with requirements for this and that, competencies and all their presumed measurements, degrees and diplomas, professional standards, approved and accepted bodies of information, and whole catalogs full of other details. And, at the end of the great, epic journey of education, in which not a few will spend as much as a quarter of a century, you should be able to do something, *one* something.

Epictetus, who could neither read nor write, supposed that education was an inner condition, easily—if temporarily—reached, in nothing more than an afternoon of thoughtful discourse, but a condition by virtue of which one could do everything that living requires, and do it well. How naive he seems, by contrast with any college's typical summer reading list for incoming freshmen. If so, it was because he shared the idea of education that was destroyed in that momentous and unnoticed historical event, the enforced separation of Goodness and Knowledge.

The two were once understood as one and the same condition, a condition that was also to be called Happiness. The three were held as intimately related as the sides of the famous right triangle, whose designation as "right" is not an accident. Somewhere, sometime, perhaps by the action of some joint committee, those ideas were cut apart and portioned out. On the one side, one faction chose Knowledge for its special kingdom, and granted Goodness to the other faction. The Knowledge people and the Goodness people made a pact, promising not to meddle in each other's business, and decided also to split Happiness down the middle, putting into the hands of the Knowledge people Happiness (and success) in this world, and into the hands of the Goodness people Happiness (and success) in another world. The meeting probably took a long time, centuries perhaps, but its plans and proposals were very successful. To this day, we do believe that Knowledge and Goodness are not only separate but very different things, and that Happiness comes in two brands, one of them easily measured, and the other, well, less easily measured, but a really great thing, if there is such a thing. (That's why the Knowledge people are just now way out in front of the Goodness people; the latter can only promise, but the former can actually deliver.)

Those important words do need some examination. Knowledge. Goodness. Happiness. And the examination of words needs some examination itself.

Philosophy, in our time, has become a very difficult study. There is quite a lot of it, and much of it is very hard to understand indeed. It is surely an important and powerful enterprise of our species—the making of philosophy—and it surely has upon us all effects of which we are not aware. I stand in awe not only of philosophers, but of professors of philosophy, for their sheer learning is tremendous, and they are habitually attentive to many little things that would help any one of us in the search for the mind's grasp of itself—the careful definition of terms, for instance.

But I have this one complaint against them, a complaint that I finally learned to express from C. S. Lewis, a man not accurately described as a philosopher, but only as a thinker. He tells the story of his own youthful embarrassment when, in conversation with friends, dons like himself, he referred to philosophy as a "subject." His friends looked away, as though pretending not to have noticed a luncheon companion slurping his soup. One of them, after a silence, reminded Lewis that for Plato, philosophy was not a subject, but a "way." Better yet, The Way.

But, the technical and mechanical requirements of schooling being what they are, the professors of philosophy, if not many of the philosophers themselves, have brought us to the belief that philosophy is indeed a subject, and not an easy one at that. And that leaves us in the belief that, if philosophy is, in fact, also a way, it is a difficult path, not only to walk, but even to find. Nowadays, it is a broad and inviting boulevard that leads us into the kind of Goodness claimed for religious belief, and were Jesus to return among us he would find it more appropriate to say, not of faith, but of philosophy, that straight is the gate, and narrow the way, and few there be that enter therein.

That's too bad. It gives us the impression that we can not for and by ourselves know the Good. It takes professional experts to do that. And when, and if, we do consult the professional experts, and what a big job that is, we discover that they do agree that the search for the Good is a highly technical enterprise suitable only for those with great knowledge, intelligence, skill, and practice in rigidly strict thinking and logical argumentation; but as to the Good, they do not agree. This leads us either to abandon the search and settle, without being certain why, on one authority rather than another, or to conclude, comfortably and conveniently, that the Good is an illusion anyway, that everything is relative after all, and it doesn't matter so long as you've got your health, which is diligently being looked after by a special branch of the very successful Knowledge faction.

How different philosophy was in an earlier time, before it became the private property of schools. People sat around and talked, but they talked not as we so often talk, at random, and by recitation. They did know and use one little trick, and that was the trick of paying attention to what is said, and equal attention to searching out the meaning of what is said. And "the meaning" of what is said they understood in a very interesting way. The meaning of what is said is what can and must be said *about* what is said.

We have a good example of that meaning of meaning in our earlier consideration of slavery, for instance. If we want to make sense when we talk about slavery, we will have to know what we mean by the term. Lacking that knowledge, we can't truly say whether we have in fact given it up, or even whether, as the assertion held, that slavery *is* in fact "antithetical to civilization," whatever *that* may mean. So now we must talk. That is truly the only way. We are looking for statements. We can easily begin with the statements that we can now make, but ahead of us, as we make statements and then make statements about our statements, there lie statements that we are *not* able to make just now. We don't *know* them. The path has not yet been trodden out that far.

We can easily begin by saying things about slavery, and the laws and customs related to it, as a political, economic, and social institution. We can ask whether slavery as an outward and visible condition is related in any way to inner and less visible attributes in people, people who are slaves, people who are masters, people who want to be slaves, people who want to be masters. And about those attributes, we can make statements. We can make statements about the outward practice of enslavement, the enslavement of others, and ask whether there might be some inward analogy to that practice, some form of self-enslavement, perhaps to passions, perhaps to unquestioned beliefs.

We can even, by the amazing power of literacy, call upon the assistance of others, long dead. When we come to consider whether slavery is indeed antithetical to civilization, maybe Socrates will drop in to tell us his wonderful story about just that consideration. He called upon his friends to imagine a prosperous and respectable citizen living in comfort in a fine little estate in town, well and dutifully served by a large staff of competent and industrious slaves. How pleasant a life. How comfortable and secure he is in all that he possesses. And now imagine, he urged his friends, that somehow, by magic, the man and his estate, his wife and children, and all his goods, along with his faithful staff of slaves, are all transported into some distant and unknown land set down far, far away from all other human beings. And there, where there are no laws, no legislature, no guardians of the civil peace, no juries, no jails, what will come to pass with that man and all that he possesses? What sort of master will he be there, and who will govern whom, and according to what law?

Having made those statements, he might ask us whether we would like to use them in our own consideration of the true relationship of slavery to civilization. We would begin to find some new and perhaps surprising statements that can and must be made.

Whether of slavery, or of Happiness, or of any other idea at all, where will such a discussion end? Will it have what is called a bottom line? Will we be able to use its answer in a multiple-choice question, so that we can test whether someone has "learned" it? To expect such things is to confuse the search for meaning with the solution of a problem. There is no place where the trains cross. There is only the journey, and it has no end. The journey itself is the answer, and the best answer we can have.

If I can not manage to solve a train problem, you can help me out and tell me the answer. If you have the patience, you can also show me what I ought to have done to find the answer for myself, but when a train problem is "real," not just cooked up as a game but a requirement for something that I have to *do* in the world, all I really need is that answer. Then I can do something. So, while there is also a "journey" in problem-solving, it is not a journey that I have to take for myself. In total and lifelong ignorance of all of the principles that make the internal combustion engine possible, I can drive a car.

In a thoughtful inquiry into meaning, everything is just the other way around. Unless I have made that journey by myself, the answer is of no use to me. It is no more than hearsay. When someone solves the problems involved in tunneling under a river, I can drive through the tunnel that he has built. But when he tells me the meaning of deeds, I have only his testimony. And even when I have inquired into the meaning of deeds, and reached some rational understanding, there is still no guarantee that I will be empowered to *do* something. I might be able, however, to *be* something that I was not before, but even that depends on my will to be something that I was not before.

Furthermore, it isn't truly *the* journey that they have made. They have done, I would more correctly say, some journeying. They have not come to the end. There is no end. If there were an end to our consideration of slavery, there would have to be, way out there, some Last Statement, some sentence about which nothing further could be said. We have as much hope of finding the Last Statement as of finding the largest possible number.

Everybody knows that, of course; everybody knows that there is no "cash value," as William James called it, in considering the meaning of ideas like slavery and Happiness. There is nothing we can get out and do after we have considered. There seems to be, therefore, nothing happening out in the world because of our considerations. It makes speculation seem vain, an esoteric exercise in cleverness that butters no bread. And many of us imagine, furthermore, that we can actually point to the "failure" of all such undertakings. Have they not been speculating and considering for thousands of years, those impractical thinkers, as to the Good, and endlessly exploring the distinction between the better and the worse? And what has come of it all? Do we now know what the Good is? Have they found for us the secret of telling right from wrong? Have they shown me, a parent who wants to rear a child in Knowledge, Goodness, and Happiness, what those things are, that I may ensure them unto her?

In other words, we complain because they have not solved any problems, and we are out of patience with them for having failed to do that which they never set out to do in the first place. They might stand on firmer ground than we, should they ask us what makes us think that the distinction between the better and the worse is in fact a "problem," that they, or anyone, might solve it, might bring home the answer and bestow it upon all humanity. They might also ask us by what reasoning we have concluded that we can have it both ways, that in one breath we can say that those remote and lofty thinkers have not answered our questions as to the good, and, in another, we can boast that "we" have indeed become a "better" species, having virtuously given up such nasty habits as slavery and dueling and cannibalism.

A friend came to Epictetus to complain that philosophy was not doing him the good he had expected. How so, asked Epictetus. Well, you see, the friend said, I have this brother-in-law, a colossal pain, and a sponger as well as an idler. I try to put it to him that he is leading a meaningless life, and severely injuring his own soul—to say nothing of mine—and that he ought to shape up and get a job. But nothing I say convinces him. He always has some smart-alec answer. So I think I need a few more lessons in how to philosophize.

Epictetus put it to him that philosophy—and he didn't mean it as a "subject" in school—was bounded by the skin. It had no power over the world. It could bring about tremendous changes, but only inside. It was not with the brother-in-law that his unhappy friend was failing, but only with himself. It is not for the persuasion of others that one studies to be better, but for the sake of being better. Indeed, as a persuader of others, the brother-in-law was clearly the stronger, for he had easily done what the would-be improver had failed to do. He had brought about an unpleasant and unvirtuous condition in somebody else, and kept his own condition, whatever it might be, intact. And would the friend prefer, then, to learn, for the sake of making his brother-in-law better, the very arts and devices by which the brother-in-law had so easily managed to make him worse?

Meanwhile, back in her tiny bedroom, Petronilla sleeps. We are still determined to rear her with an eye to Knowledge, Goodness, and Happiness. We do not know for certain what those things are, and even if we did, we could not tell her. First of all, because she is asleep. All children are asleep, more or less, which suggests yet another way of defining children. But, and far more important, we could not tell her even if she were awake. In such matters, there is no telling. If there were, we wouldn't have to trouble ourselves to think and consider. We could look it up. There is only the journeying. If she is to do that journeying, under our guidance, we will have to do it, and thus learn, not *the* path, or *the* destination, but journeying itself.

Listen now to the voices of three possible parents of Petronilla, any one of whom is also probable:

First Parent: I am in favor of Knowledge, Goodness, and Happiness, and I certainly do want them for my child. I am aware, however, that no one has been able to say exactly what those things are, and that by now it seems clear that no one ever will. It would be a waste of time and effort for me to pretend to bring all those considerations to a conclusion, so I will just have to hope for the best, and look around for some good examples or ideas that seem to work for somebody, and, of course, whenever possible, urge her to be good and learn things. I'll also see what makes her happy and try to provide as much of it as possible, provided, of course, that it won't also have the effect of making her bad, or, come to think of it, of keeping her in ignorance. Hmm. Maybe that won't always be so easy. It looks as though I may have to do some guessing as I go along. Well, I am going to be very sincere, and I am going to try very hard to do the right thing, and maybe it will all work out for the best. There. That's my plan.

Second Parent: I know what Goodness consists of, and I know that Happiness comes from being good. Frankly, I'm not at all sure that Knowledge has much to do with either. I know lots of very smart and well-informed people who seem to be less good than they ought to be just *because* of all that Knowledge, and who, furthermore, do not agree with me as to the nature of Goodness. I will simply see to it that this child does agree with me. I will just tell her.

Third Parent: Now that I think about it for a minute, I'm not at all sure that I have ever made any distinctions between Happiness and Pleasure, for instance. Or between Knowledge and Information. Should I rear this child as though there were no differences? And what about Goodness? Is that the same thing as Obedience? Or as Conformity? Wouldn't that depend on what was to be obeyed, or conformed to? I suspect that I can never know for certain what any of those things actually *are*, but I do have to do something about deciding what, in this case, they ought to be. It's a good thing the child is still asleep, because it looks as though I have some work to do before she wakes up and starts asking questions. I think I had better begin with talking to myself for a while. Maybe I'll start with something that sounds particularly intriguing. Pleasure. I wonder, do *I* mean the same thing by Pleasure as I do by Happiness? Is Pleasure good, or is some Pleasure good and another bad? If I could decide which is which, what would I have, Knowledge or Information? Well, I can see that this is going to take a while. I'd better get to it.

It is not difficult to choose which parent you would prefer if you happened to be Petronilla. Is it any more difficult to choose which parent you would like to be?

Petronilla is in some danger. How will it come to pass with her if she has drawn the wrong parent? How likely is she to come some day into the grasp of her own mind, to wake up, if she is the child of the second parent, or even of the first parent? Will she not have to depend on luck alone?

Well, that's the way it is, we all know. Lots of people just have to depend on luck. We can't save them all. For one thing, we can't even find them all. How can we know the hearts of all parents, and the measure of every child's peril? Who are we to judge, and say of this one that he is the first parent, and of that one that he is the second parent? There is only one case in which you have the resources to make such a judgment. In yourself. If you have chosen the parent that you would rather be, consider now the parent that you are. If some of the details don't exactly fit, change them. And, having done that, look around and see if you can find Petronilla. Unless you are astonishingly unusual, Petronilla is somewhere in you, sleeping soundly. Of *that* Petronilla, you can not say that she will just have to take her chances along with everybody else. If she never comes to take the grasp of her own mind, it will not be for lack of luck, but because you, who could have provided a design where the world can provide only happenstance, chose not to do that. You know her, and you know her parent, and you know what ought to be done.

EIGHT

SAD STORIES
of the
DEATH
of
KINGS

THE STRANGE POWER THAT WE
call imagination is at once a form of thinking and a useful aid
to more thinking. Imagination can be understood as at once
a kind of intelligence and a kind of poetry, which we ordinarily think of as something not at all intellectual but "creative." A bad mistake. Poetry and intelligence have one
tremendous power in common. Each is a way of discovering, and of revealing, that things very different from each
other are also like each other, and that similar things are very
different from each other. Metaphor is in the heart of each,
some way of language that can treat a city seen at dawn in
the distance as though it were a sleeping creature and a girl
as though she were a rose.

It is mind that does such things, of course, and if that way
of understanding is to be called creative, then we might better understand human "creativity" not as some unaccountable and maybe emotional urge within, but as thinking. As
such, it is remarkably useful in the mind's work of knowing
itself.

My mind to me, a kingdom is, says the poet. Well, that's
nice. It is hardly one of the great, sonorous lines of mighty
verse, but it does stay in the mind. And we can think about
it, which might be better than "appreciating" it, whatever
that might mean. It would be fun to have the poet here, to
ask him some questions about his curious assertion, and
even to consider whether or not he has gone a bit too far.
Can it be that what he says is simply a truthful description of
some might and majesty, or is he perhaps boasting a little
about his independent, sensitive, poetic mind? And, an even
more important question: Is he doing his proper duty as a
poet, and casting light on some universal by example of the
particular, or is he just "expressing himself"?

So, your mind is a kingdom, eh? What sort of a kingdom
is it? Are the borders open or jealously guarded? Do the citizens rejoice in their king, his just laws, and his kind gover-
nance, or do they have to console themselves with the

thought that someday they will get to die and escape all this? Are the king's officers arrogant or cordial in the execution of their duties? Do they take bribes?

And how about the politics of your little kingdom? Is there a perpetual feud going on between the conservatives and the liberals? Is the king himself the king of all, or is he the leader of one of the factions? Is he in secure possession of his throne, or is he beset by pretenders? Is there any danger of revolution? Which side would you be on?

A poet, of course, would probably find such questions diverting, and worth some playful consideration. No, no, this one would probably say, the borders of my land are welcoming and open. Merchants and princes and sages bring treasures from afar. The land is thus full of beauty and light, which the king loves more than power and might. And I do suspect that he meant, by the word "kingdom," some immense combination of a well-tended park and a well-stocked museum, probably not caring much about that one essential which makes one kingdom one sort of place, and another, quite a different sort of place. And that is Politics.

Aristotle held, and Plato too, and many others, that the highest and most important study to which we could devote ourselves is the thoughtful consideration of politics. An extraordinarily dreary prospect for most of us, who suppose that it is Politics that we see in action in election campaigns, and in all the unseemly scramble for office and power. But that is not at all what ancient thinkers meant by the word. For them, Politics, this time with the capital, was the study of "polity," the consideration of questions about the art and nature of virtuous governing, and the inquiry into the possibility of a just state. It was not really about what we call *the government*, except insofar as this or that government might serve as an example, but about *governing*, and it was not confined to considerations of the state and its workings, but gave itself also to considering the just governing of anything or anyone. It was thus yet another way of self-knowledge, for the self is, just as much as the state, a place, and even a community, and it may, just like the state, be governed well or ill.

While it looks tame, a schoolteacher's work can also be dangerous. A professor is, supposedly, one who "professes" something, who holds something both true and worthy, not merely correct and useful. The act of professing, therefore, arises at least partly from a condition that might correctly be called "loyalty," and it is presumably out of the recognition that something *deserves* loyalty that a professor has chosen to profess. Thus, the special sin that always lies in wait for those who profess is treachery, the withdrawal of loyalty from that to which it had once been freely granted, and granted neither out of sentiment nor practicality, but out of recognition of merit.

None of that is mentioned, of course, in the oath taken by professors as they enter into their callings, because there is no such oath. Professors do not even, like physicians, promise aloud and in public that they will "first of all, do no harm." Thus it is that there is not, among professors, a great central theme to which all, whatever their special corners of interest, have given thoughtful and willing assent, as there is among physicians the great theme of healing. In the lack of any public oath, it seems only decent for a professor to devise and utter a private one, and its first clause might well be, for it will apply equally to professors of philosophy and professors of media management, *"Primum, non mentior."* First of all, to tell no lies. For just as surely as harm is the very opposite of healing, and thus the physician's veriest adversary, the lie is the very opposite of what the professor is given to seek. Truth. Of course, for those who do not admit the existence of Truth, there is no lying, and they would have to devise some other oath. Or do without.

I do hold, for instance, that in the readings that I study and consider with my students, there is Truth, the continual search for the truest possible understandings of how it is with us humans. All good books are, whatever else they may be, the recorded work of some mind trying to take the grasp of itself, trying to bring into order the random and accidental universe of experience, and thus to find meaning. And to tell it, but to tell it not as a problem's solution may be told, not as a "moral" or a bottom line, but as a grand metaphor, whose very boundaries are marked not by barriers but by signposts pointing outward and beyond.

Any truthful literature will admit: No, this is not life itself, it is only a serious sort of game, but it is like life, and the mind that plays here is like yours, and this vision is what you too can see, and consider, and find worthy, and by which you may know yourself better. For this book is about you. Every truthful and thoughtful book is about you, every story is yours.

My outbursts of treachery occur when I come to believe, or pretend that I believe, that literature is all a lie. Those so-called Great Books come to seem the highly specialized productions of exceedingly few people, elegant exercises of the elite, having nothing to do with humanity in general. I begin to imagine the little-suspected existence among us of the Great Mind Club, an outfit even more exclusive than Mensa, whose members are truly a race apart, not like us, and whose conversations we can, at best, overhear, but into whose lives and minds, integrally united in a way that mine seems never to be, we can not truly enter. And their quaint notions of the Good, the True, and the Beautiful seem the stuff of elfin fantasies and dreams, charming whimsies for the idle hour between productive labor and sleep.

In those times, my students, although entirely innocent, seem to provide some new evidence to contradict the deepest theme not only of all literature but of all concerted and deliberate thoughtfulness, which is that the temporary and particular are always outward and visible signs of whatever is permanent and universal. There are times—I suspect every teacher knows them—when I can not for the life of me detect in some of my students any hint whatsoever of the permanent and universal. They seem to me not what they truly are, the legitimate sons and daughters—and heirs as well—of all the great and nourishing spirits from the time of the astonishing painters of the walls of caves right down to yesterday. They seem, rather, some new life form, with no past, recently come among us, and utterly without those qualities that humanity has always supposed to be its essentials, the unique qualities by which a person is a person, not only *not another* sort of creature, but not any other person either.

They seem to find no beauty in the Beautiful, and Truth and Goodness do not especially interest them. They give no sign of a desire to know. They seem not to have dreamed of even the *possibility* of actually examining and judging the life that they live. And, should they glimpse it, the prospect does not please them. It is as though they were synthetic, the dish-cultured product of some secret laboratory operated by demented bioengineers.

Straightaway I grow cynical and negligent, thinking of Saint Anthony preaching to the fishes, and pitying myself all the more to remember that the fishes did at least listen to the Saint, and even approve his words, for a while. It is a disgusting and childish condition, and I have, at last, learned to recover from it and do better work by bringing my students into some consideration of the topic that seems so dreary, stale, and even tacky—Politics. Thus, I recover my loyalty through seeking in them the permanent and universal, and always finding it. They truly are, and by nature, it seems, political, carrying in the minds that seem so empty the very ideas of good and virtuous government to which the ancients urged us all to attend.

Plato seems to have concluded that the idea of Justice is not one that we have to learn, but that we have it by Nature. As evidence, we can cite the fact that even little children can tell the difference between fairness and unfairness, and are quick to point it out, however privately. I'm not entirely convinced by that fact, because I'm not sure that it *is* a fact. It seems to me rather that little children, just like you and me, are very good at detecting only certain cases of Injustice, and have a way of not noticing it when they don't happen to think themselves its victims. If there is something innate in us, therefore, I am inclined to suspect that it is not our recognition of Justice for what it is, but our incessant wanting, which is very quiet when satisfied but noisy when thwarted. No matter. I do not, in order to do my work, have to answer that ancient question as to whether anything at all can be innate in us. By the time I look for the idea of Justice in my students, it is there. That will do.

Even a mistaken complaint against Injustice is an appeal to principle. No one says, Your treatment of me is wrong *because* I don't like it. Everyone calls upon some "higher power," which finds that treatment wrong *in itself*, whether anyone likes it or not. Someday, someone will say, What you propose to do in my case is surely well-intended and would please me a lot, but I must ask you to refrain, for it would not be just. Diogenes will blow out his lamp and go home to bed. Nevertheless, the latter complaint is alive and well in the former, and who makes the one can be led to see Reason in the other. When my students notice unfairness, I notice that they are human, and hope returns, and loyalty with it, for I know that any one of them could, just *could*, send Diogenes home someday.

I do not mean by that the fact that they have adopted, willy-nilly, this or that party affiliation, although they usually have. I mean something deeper, the impulse that perhaps brings us all so naturally to join this or that party of opinion, by which we intend, however inarticulately or ineffectively, or even mistakenly, to serve nothing less than Justice. And my students, even the most lazy and self-indulgent—I might better say *especially* the most lazy and self-indulgent—are interested in Justice. They are more than interested; they are *for* it. They know that it is good, and Injustice, bad. That knowledge is the root of Politics and of our concerns with goodness in government, both the outer government of the state and the inner government of the mind.

All I have to do so that they will *know* themselves as inquirers into Justice, is to have them read *Antigone*. When they have done that, I ask them whether they remember especially any certain line or passage. It's a gamble, but I usually win, and not by luck, but because I know that they are interested in Justice, and *for* it. And the passage that someone can always be counted on to choose is the one in which Haemon is dismissed by his father, Creon the king, as too young to question the wisdom of his elders. But if I happen to be right, answers the son, what does my age matter? That, every student, of whatever persuasion, or color, or I.Q., or previous condition of ignorance, understands. That may be only a first step, but it is *the* step that must be taken first. Refinements can come later.

Literature is always about Justice, about truth and falsehood, about harm and healing. It is always about the transactions between persons, which are the only possible dwelling places of Justice and Injustice. There is no more Injustice in earthquakes than there is Justice in sunny skies, for Justice comes of choosing, and there must be a chooser. Literature is about persons choosing, or failing to choose, or not knowing how or why to choose, and about the world that such persons make, and in which other persons must live. Every book is a portrayal of a kingdom, a system of related persons living in a land whose borders are the first and last pages. That land has its Politics.

That is why some wandering around in the kingdoms of literature is essential to a true education. It has nothing to do with "culture," with the presumed social advantages that accrue to those who can recognize, or even use in just the right place, a line from *The Taming of the Shrew*. And it is not for the sake of "appreciating" the great works, which, in practice, can mean nothing more than feeling, or claiming to feel, some traditionally approved sentiment in the presence of Goethe and Flaubert. And it is useful as a ticket of admission to our "common heritage" only if that common heritage is understood not as the library of this or that historical tradition or culture, but as the permanent reservoir of everything that makes us *all* human, in all times, and in all places.

The difference between that literature most suitable for "children," whatever that might mean, and that most suitable for "grown-ups," whom we will be able to identify once we have identified the children, is this: Children learn what they most need to know from happy stories of the birth of kings, and grown-ups learn again and again what they most need to remember from sad stories of the death of kings. The birth of the king is the coming into the world of Justice, and the death of the king is its passing. In the birth of the king, children recognize the Right, and in his death, grown-ups recognize the Wrong, and, having been children, know where to look for the return of the Right.

Everybody remembers the famous story of the Princess and the Frog, and its happy outcome. Give yourself a little test on that story. It is not a test of "intelligence." Who was it that brought about that happy outcome, and how? It was not the frog, who is, after all, strictly speaking, a monster, a monster *pro tem*, to be sure, but still a monster. It was not the princess, who is, after all, a child, a child *pro tem*, to be sure, but still a child. It was the only grown-up in the tale, who is not only the father of the princess, but the king. And a just king.

When the princess returns to the table, saying that there was no one at the door, her father knows that she is lying. He requires of her the truth, and then says:

Listen, young lady, your rank gives you not privileges but responsibilities. To be royal is to be "right." A false princess is no princess at all. We do not break our given word. We do not abandon those who helped us in our need. Do you now go down to the door and let that frog in and treat him as you ought.

And the result is that on the very next day, the princess, now a queen, goes off with a king, newly reborn out of unnatural monstrosity, to rule in her own land. And that, all the stories tell us, the stories for children and the stories for grown-ups as well, is the goal of this life—to rule in one's own land. It is the goal of education as well, and equally the goal set for us by Prometheus, for to rule in one's own land can mean, for each and every one of us, nothing different from the mind's grasp of itself as the informer and the director of the will.

There is an important difference between that story and a story that we looked at earlier. The king assumes that the princess is nothing but a child, and must be taught by precept; Jesus assumes that the accusers are the strangely double creatures that most of us are, children here and there and now and then, but also, if in moments only, grown-ups who can be taught by a very different process, and a process that has, significantly, no convenient name among us, and which I have had to call, for lack of a more descriptive term, the "occasion of education."

What a risk he took. Suppose that those accusers had been completely and only children. Suppose they had been utterly under the control of their appetites, and incapable of self-government by any means; with no thoughtful grasp of their own minds, and unable to "talk about goodness," to give thoughtful consideration as to what they believed, and as to whether they ought to believe it. Stones would have been thrown that day.

He sent them into their minds, each into his own kingdom, and told them to learn to bring it into order and to rule it, and not to be ruled by any foreign power. And each one declared independence. Each declaration of independence was a political act, committed after having asked and answered certain familiar questions. Who is competent to rule, and by virtue of what? How shall the realm live, by the force of feelings, or by the dictation of beliefs that can never rise to the rank of Knowledge, but take their strength from custom and tradition, and not from Reason? Who is to decide, in this land, what is the Good, and to live by it without regard to comfort or profit or the approval of the emissaries of other lands? Those are the questions that lead to the drawing up of a constitution, or the coronation of a just king, if one of those can be found.

In a person, there is a community, a society. There are many voices. They are all parts of the self, some immigrants for the world out there, and some the native-born, the remnants of earlier selves, which never go away. The little child I once was, I still may be at any moment, either delighting in some fresh wonder as though Beauty had appeared in the world for the first time, or whining for favor and pleasure. And then there's that teenager, and his only slightly older alter ego who knows everything. The *dramatis personae* are countless, and, while few are on the stage in any given scene, they are all waiting, some of them panting, in the wings. They all hold the script, to say nothing of the plot, in the deepest contempt, barging on stage whenever they please. And, while the turmoil they cause is quite enough to make life, over and over again, into a tale told by an idiot, signifying nothing, far behind them there lurks the constant threat of the Great Idiot himself, skulking in the subbasements like the Phantom of the Opera, and waiting for his chance. You know him as well as I do. He is the one who suddenly appears at center stage and takes over completely when you discover a tarantula in the glove compartment. The Idiot is in charge when you fall into rage, or panic, or utterly into appetite.

Who can direct these actors? How shall these citizens be governed? If the land is to have order, and the plot, meaning, who is to be at once their author and king? Can their proper roles be found, and can they be brought to play them, so that each can contribute usefully both to the health of the body politic and to the theme of the piece? Will some of them just have to go, incurable sociopaths beyond all hope of rehabilitation? And who can send them away? After all, they can all claim to have been born here, and they all know that they have their rights.

Such a state of affairs makes a sad story indeed, and it is all the sadder because the king seems to be dead. There is no one in charge. Accident and happenstance spin the plot. It is as though my life were a story being written by no one, but also by anyone, or anything. It has no consistent theme, and not even a clearly identifiable main character. Which of this motley crew is me? Do I have a choice? Who is the chooser? What will the others say, and, even worse, what will they do next?

Those are all political questions, questions about government. That it happens to be my own government makes the answers not less important but actually more important than the equivalent answers for the land in which I live. A citizen who governs himself but poorly, to say nothing of a citizen who will not govern himself at all, lays upon his fellows not only the terrible burden of doing what he could do for himself but won't, but also the temptation, often, indeed, the necessity, to resort to coercion and violence. In that degree to which I am unable to govern myself, I become to you exactly the opposite of the "occasion of education," for you will be driven, in handling me, to choose something other than Reason.

And my self-government is more important than "the government" for another reason. About the latter, I can do almost nothing, and that "almost" is only a quibble. About the former, I can do something. Will I? Even about the willing, I can do something. Perhaps if I stop to think about some Petronilla, whose own powers of self-government will

131

depend on mine, I might strengthen even my obstinate will. And if I go on to think about my own child, the whining brat that interrupts some of my best scenes and writes his own script by lung power alone, and remember that unless I can govern him all the rest of you will have to, and in a way that I may find as unpleasant as he will surely find it, I may suddenly discover that self-government and self-interest are sometimes happily served at once. That should make it easier.

All I need is a good king.

The examples of the world, however, will not provide one. The kings of this world are just like me, and perhaps even a bit worse off, owing, for kings, a surprising amount of obedience to all sorts of powers and pressures outside of themselves. Plato once took a job with a king, Dionysius of Syracuse, who had been his student. He wanted to test whether wise and just government could be established out there in the world. The result was bad. And poor Voltaire, even knowing what had happened to Plato, undertook to make the philosopher-king out of the amiable and enlightened Frederick the Great. The result was bad.

As to the government of the self, however, there is no shortage of models, not in the kings of the world, but in the kings of the mind. We have all seen them, and we can all recognize them for what they are.

NINE

HOME RULE

T HERE ARE SUCH NOURISHING
and reasonable, and even obvious, ways of describing and
understanding education, and then pursuing it, that some
strange species of credit must be given to our schoolers, who
have ingeniously concocted countless other ways that are de-
bilitating, silly, and unlikely. Then, having made themselves
an unlovely idol, and bowing down before it, they have licensed themselves as nothing but "realistic" in its service, as
though it were simply part of the world, and not of their
own making. So too, somebody's notion of intelligence is
granted the rank of "reality" and the power to bind us all.

But education, like intelligence, is not a thing in the
world, and what it "is" is, truly, nothing more than a "manner of speaking." It is what we say it is, and what we say it is
comes not from a process that might be called "discovery,"
but from invention. We make it. Accordingly, you do not
have to listen to anybody else. You can say for yourself what
education is, and what you say is not subject to the judgment of those who say something else, but only to the judgment of Reason. If they say something else by the power of
demonstrable Reason, then you should pay attention, but
otherwise, they are talking rubbish, and deserve no attention
at all. The first and most obvious understanding of education comes from the fact that anyone who can not tell Reason from rubbish is not yet in a condition to know that he
can not tell Reason from rubbish, a disability which, you
would suppose, can hardly be one of those put forth as education. But it is.

For your own purposes, and for the sake of Petronilla,
which is really the same thing, consider the consequences of
adopting, as an understanding of education, the ability to tell
rubbish from Reason. Nothing more. Nothing but the
power, and the propensity, to discover that a statement is
worthless, or a term without meaning, or a proposition ab-
surd. That would also be the power to make statements that
are *not* worthless, and propositions that make demonstrable

sense. That seems little enough to ask, although a moment's reflection will suggest that it is far more than it looks, and perhaps far more than we can imagine. But consider also the alternative of your adoption of such an understanding of education. Would you be willing to hold, as it seems to me that our general understanding of education does in fact hold, that the condition called "education" does *not* require the ability to tell rubbish from Reason, but only some powers by which to get along in the world?

From Epictetus, we can take another possible understanding of education. It is power over the inner world, the ability to know and judge the self and to do something about it. It is not, therefore, the same as whatever it is that gives us power over the outer world, the stubborn public world of Nature and Necessity. The two powers neither preclude each other nor include each other. In any mind, either may exist alone, both may exist, and, of course, in any mind, both may be absent.

The two powers are not exactly equal counterparts, however, for the power over the inner world can make judgment of the power over the outer world. By the latter, we can do something; by the former, we can decide whether we *should* do what we can do.

Should we, in fact, destroy most of the world and its people, future generations might say of us:

They did what they could. They did anything and everything they could. They seem to have had no way of knowing, and were not especially interested in asking, whether they *should* do whatever they could.

The ability to know and judge the self may seem a rather minimal, and, to some, even a selfish and antisocial definition of education, but imagine instead some understanding of education from which it is excluded. Such an understanding is what is stuck in our heads by popular beliefs about schooling. Out of it, we suppose that a brain surgeon—why is it always brain surgeons?—is educated. And we suppose the same, but without expecting to pay as much for it, of our teachers and professors, especially of those who have stuck us with the idea that education *is* the power to work change in the outer world of Nature and Necessity. And then we say that it is all those overeducated theorists and physicists who are going to blow us all up.

And then there is the understanding of education with which I began, education as that which makes us able to be good. Able. A disarming proposition. Who can be against the ability to be good? Granted, the ability is only that, and easily permits us to imagine someone who is perfectly capable of being good but would rather not. Nevertheless, there is nothing "mere" about the ability, for without it there is no hope of goodness at all.

Those three views of education all hang together. Indeed, they are only slightly different views of the same quality or power. Not one of them could exist without the others. He who has no reliable way of telling rubbish from Reason can have no knowledge of the self that he is to judge and control, by which judgment, and only by which judgment, he is able to choose the better over the worse. It will not only be the voice of the world that deceives him; his own voice will deceive him. As to his own beliefs and propositions, which may not even be his own, but only his recitations of what the world says, he will not be able to tell rubbish from Reason. That condition, however, need not hinder his effectiveness in bringing about changes in the outer world. He may be perfectly capable of what is nowadays called "excellence," which is the new name for a particularly visible combination of efficiency and success, a high and measurable degree of effectiveness in problem-solving. It has to do with such things as the marketing of blow dryers, in which sort of enterprise the words "better" and "worse" have not the same meanings as they had for the men who didn't throw stones.

To most people, those understandings of education seem at once lofty and insipid, idealistic and impractical, however "noble." And that is precisely because they do not include problem-solving. If Western culture had had such understandings of education for the last two thousand years, would we now be flying through the air at twice the speed of sound? Would we be sending men to pick up rocks on the moon? Would we have conquered polio and diphtheria? Would we have air conditioners and blenders? Or even matches? Would we have, as the author of *Missile Envy* asserts, "the secret of atomic energy locked in our heads forever"?

I don't know the answers to such questions. Nobody knows them. Some questions are interesting and important because of the answers to which they lead, and others are interesting and important because of what they say about those who ask them. The questions above are of the second kind. To ask them at all, we have to make some astonishing assumptions.

They are all asked in the Land of We All. Only out of a great delusion would I say, We have learned how to send men to pick up rocks on the moon. No such thing is true. We have not. Somebody has, to be sure, but not "we." We have not wiped out polio, nor have we learned the secret of atomic energy. A few of us, and a very few of us, have done all such things. Unless I remember that, I am continually subject to the delusion that tells me that *I* am somehow "better" and more "advanced" than my very distant ancestors who painted pictures on the walls of caves, and just because I happen to be a member of we.

Ah, I say, those poor, ignorant savages. They could paint, all right, no one denies that, even Picasso said so, but what is painting? It's some sort of gift, I guess, and they were lucky to have it. But could they even do so simple a thing as make fire? No. They had to find it, and then preserve it carefully. I, on the other hand, to name only the very least of my accomplishments, can make fire just like that! Whenever I please. I can, with a tiny movement of a finger, bring light into a dark place, and the very images and voices of distant sportscasters right into the room where I sit. Even these tri-fling powers, to say nothing at all of internal combustion and refrigeration, bear witness to the progress that comes of problem-solving, and to the betterment of all humanity.

But I am deluded. I can not make fire any better than the cave painter of twenty thousand years ago. Indeed, I can not make fire at all, having failed that requirement of Cub Scouting along with the tying of the sheepshank. What I can do is strike a match, but I can not even claim to strike a match any better than he would have struck a match, had he had one. I can not make a match any more than he could have made a match. I can flip a light switch no better than he could have, but I can not make the enormous system that makes the light switch work, or even any small part of it, although I may sometimes be able to rewire the switch without stabbing myself with a screwdriver. I can buy my ticket and board a plane, and I can pay my taxes toward the work of those few who *can* send men to the moon to pick up rocks, and who *do* have the secret of atomic energy in their heads, but that's it. I am, in every one of the "great advance-ments of mankind," as we understand them, a sort of pas-senger, a freeloader at that. I have not been a party to any one of them. I am along for the ride. And, while I gladly take whatever "profit" comes from the work of a very few, I must also take whatever "loss" may just as often come from that work. And the same is true of almost everybody else, including those very few who do all such things. The one who has the secret of atomic energy locked in his head does not have all of the secret. He needs some other very few. Nor can he wipe out diphtheria, nor make fire.

What *is* there that he can do any more than I, or any more than our common ancestor who painted the walls of the caves? What is there that all three of us can do equally well, or ill? Leaving aside the particulars—the secret of atomic energy on the one hand, and the secret of yellow ochre on the other, neither of which I happen to share—what is *the* difference by virtue of which I suppose myself somehow "advanced" beyond some "worse" condition in the cave painter?

The details, I admit, seem important. I would prefer not to trade lives with the cave painter, although I'm not sure how much that means, for I would prefer not to trade lives with *anybody*. I am likely to live longer. I like that. But I have not understood any principle, except for my liking of it, by which to know that a long life is better than a short one, or even by which to decide what long and short might mean in that context. I am vexed by wanting a life that is at least "long enough," but by not being able to say what it ought to be long enough *for*. The cave painter may have had the same vexation.

I have certain comforts that the cave painter did not have. I will—perhaps—suffer less pain, unless it is one of the disadvantages of a longer life that it provides more time for the possibility of pain. And it does occur to me that, as I sit here in no pain at all, some not inconsiderable number of my contemporaries are suffering every bit as much pain as any ancient cave painter ever suffered, and asking themselves exactly what principle it is by which a long life is thought better than a short life. And of fear, the same is true. Indeed, if there really are people who live in active and continual fear of the threatened nuclear holocaust, a fear of a particularly modern kind, do they also suppose that "we" represent some sort of "improvement" over our ancestors, and that our lives are, in any deeply important sense, better?

Did the cave painter dream of me as I do of him? Did he say, Someday, my descendants will not have to lead the short, nasty, and brutish life that has fallen to my lot. Someday, they will fly through the air at great speed to attend sales conventions in distant cities, which I, alas, can not do, and buy their yellow ochre in neat little tubes. Their teeth will not rot and fall out, and most of their children will live. I, in my bad time, must struggle daily against not just hunger, but starvation, suffering pains and fears that they will never know.

The only differences between his life and mine that I can be sure of are details and particulars, differences of the outer world that now changes so quickly, and, in his time probably seemed a permanent reality. What differences can I suppose in the inner world, the world of the mind? What does his Petronilla face that mine does not, aside from the particulars? That question I am willing to answer, because I know, and you do too, what is sure to befall in every life, provided only, by a troubling sort of irony, that it is a life that is "long enough."

These things lie in wait for Petronilla, any Petronilla ever born: Pain. Vexation. Disappointment. Anger. Humiliation. Loss. Sorrow. Fear. Sickness. Bewilderment. Grief. Death. The list is partial. For me, and you, and for the cave painter alike, they are all certain. Only the details will be different. In the grip of those certainties, I will take no more advantage from my ability to fly through the air than the cave painter will take disadvantage from his inability to fly through the air, and in no *important* way will I be able to think myself "advanced" beyond him.

I have to confess that, in the years I have spent as a schoolteacher, I have learned much more from my students than they have from me. While that will surely sound like a feigned humility, it isn't feigned, and it isn't humility either. If it is a less than worthy thing to say, it is because it exhibits my presumption that I am more *able* to learn than my students. In any case, the same things happen to them and to me. We're all there. We all read and hear the same words. But the same things don't always happen *in* them and *in* me.

We often read, for such is the proper business of literature, works that deal with Happiness, with our search for it, with our loss of it, even with our finding of it. My students are keenly interested in Happiness. They want it and seek it, without being ashamed of either, for they deem the wanting and the seeking legitimate, by which they mean, Good. They are not impressed by intellectual speculations as to whether and when we *should* be happy. While they have been led to believe that the point of life is to make the world a better place for *other* people, most of them not yet born, they do not truly believe that their own deliberate choice of the life of contentious altruism will actually have that effect. They are, it seems to me, wiser than I. They would not need, as Alyosha did, and as I do, the gentle encouragement of Father Zossima, who reminds us that Happiness is our proper destiny, and that we ought not to be ashamed of wanting it, or feel guilty for finding it. And those same students prove themselves wiser still when they sometimes decide to reject Happiness.

In the study of literature, discussions of Happiness and its worth are inevitable. I find, whenever I can, an opportunity to offer the students perpetual Happiness. Suppose, I say, it were in my power, or someone's power, to grant that. Suppose there were a pill. Swallow it, and never again know a moment's unhappiness. Would you take it?

There really are some rewards in the schoolteacher business. One of mine is the fact that no one, even when pressed and cajoled, has ever said Yes to that question. On the day when someone does, I will have to conclude that I have at last found the one human being on the face of the Earth for whom there is no hope of education. But I do not expect that.

They can all easily see, especially fresh from the reading with which I have loaded the dice, that the goodness of Happiness is related to the appropriateness of Happiness, and that Happiness where Happiness is not *in order*, is a bad thing, not a good one. They know, having been spared no more than anyone else, that they will suffer misery again, but they know too that misery will someday be in order, and that one who is happy when misery is in order is not quite human. And they know that Creon the king is wretched at the end of the story, stricken by nothing less than terminal misery, and that his condition is nevertheless truly a good one, for he has become better. Nor do they see him as merely punished, properly chastised for his earlier disorder. They see him as improved, sane where he was mad, just where he was unjust. They see that his unhappiness is *in order*, and that it is the natural consequence of his earlier monstrosity, which was a neglect of order, and the substitution of his private desire for the rational Justice to which a just king is supposed to be a voluntary servant.

I am writing to you, obviously, as though I knew that you knew Sophocles' *Antigone*. I don't know that, of course. But I write thus anyway for two resons. If you don't know *Antigone,* you do know an equivalent. The same story is in *Lear.* Every classical tragedy is an equivalent, and so is every serious book. They are all about deeds in order and deeds out of order, and the great and terrible power by which order reestablishes itself, bringing the tragedy that is also a cleansing, and replacing some condition that was wrong with another that is right. So, even if you don't know the story, you know the story.

My other reason is this: I am also thinking about a story that we all know, but that no one of us knows. For I do suspect that our distant ancestor, the cave painter, knew just such a story, and that he heard it often, and, in his turn, told it often to his Petronilla. Whether she grew up in the habit of discussing it, I don't know. I doubt it. Among the particulars in which our time is indeed different from hers is the fact that we have found the free time in which to sit around discussing, and have, perhaps, brought ourselves into the *need* of discussing, which is the only recourse of those who don't understand. Nevertheless, I am ready to guess that that pre-historic Petronilla would be remarkably like my students in some very important way.

And in some trivial ways, too. Petronilla would not be able to locate the Atlantic Ocean or the Rocky Mountains on a map. Likewise, some of my students. Petronilla would know of no principle by which to figure out whether the Protestant Reformation came before or after the American Revolution. Likewise, some of my students. Petronilla would be baffled, and even amazed, by the proposition that in any collection of randomly chosen numbers there will always be an underlying principle by which the next logical number will be generated. Likewise, some of my students. Petronilla will suppose that if two men assert exactly oppo-site propositions, that one of them must be right and the other wrong. Likewise, some of my students. Petronilla will not know how to find the area of a rectangle. Likewise, some of my students. However, like all of my students, Pe-tronilla will know that Creon is a bad man at the beginning of the story and a good man at the end. She will have heard his story before, and found in it the echo of what she knew without knowing that she knew it.

She will, thus, like my students, be able to make a truly kingly judgment. It is a royal act to put aside natural desire and to decide that some condition that we don't *want* might nevertheless be a truly better condition than one that pleases us. It is not the act of a child who is governed by appetite, but the act of a grown-up who can govern appetite. It re-quires a knowledge of what is *in order* and what is not. And it brings *into* order, if only for a while, the inner world that is the mind. It is surely the power that Prometheus had in mind to give us.

It seems to me that no human being born was standing behind the door when that gift was handed out. I conclude that from the fact that I have never encountered a student so mindless as to want the perpetual happiness pill. If the thoughtful life, which alone deserves the name of true education, calls for the ability to distinguish Reason from rubbish, the ability to know and judge the self and to do something about it, and the ability to distinguish the better from the worse, then I have never found a student who was not a candidate for the thoughtful life. It seems to be the ability, the likelihood, the propensity, the wiring, as it were, that makes human beings human beings.

It is the popular view, of course, that everyone can be "educated" in something or other and to some degree or other. By that, we mean that some can aspire to brain surgery—there it is again—and others to accountancy or automobile repair. But all of these "meanings" are related not to what is the same in all of us, but to the countless and accidental attributes that are different in all of us. In all of us, mind is mind. Education does not provide the mind with newly invented powers; it is possible only because certain powers are in the mind from the start. I'm tempted to say, and will say, that it is, like language, which grows out of a power that is there from the start, not just possible, but inevitable.

But, again like language, it can be stunted, so that some Petronilla here and there can always be found in whom the power of language is small, and in whom the power of the mind is accordingly small. Although it is not routinely understood in this way, thought is talk. What we think, like what we know, or imagine that we know, exists in the form of sayings. And sayings about our sayings. When the power of saying is small, the power of thinking is small. An obvious example is visible in the simple fact that of those things for which we have no words, we can not think. If our words are few, we can say little. And if our words are mostly the words of communication, those words that name publicly visible things and events, then we can make sayings that are mostly ways of pointing to something. We have not the words to make sayings *about* our sayings. And, even more

important, we have not the words with which to make sayings about the sayings that others say to us.

I am, like you or Petronilla, considerably outnumbered by
others. Their massed voices are loud, and every one of them
is, and has to be, a foreign influence in my own kingdom.
To which of them shall I attend, and why? Which of them
have I heeded, without testing and considering them, and
performing on them what might be called acts of education,
looking to distinguish between rubbish and Reason, and between better and worse? How can I rule in my own kingdom without having done that?

The practice of Reason is the secret of home rule, but it
would be an imprudent king who neglected foreign policy
and the defense of the realm. Every border is threatened by
wandering bands and smugglers, and *agents provocateurs,* and
single spies, and thoroughly regimented armies as well; and
the higher his tower, the farther a king can see. I think that
Epictetus was right, and that true education, which he called
philosophy, has power only within, but that is also the
power to understand and judge whatever comes in from
the world outside. True education is not an adjustment to
the world, but a defense against the world, and those who
would have it must know the world as best they can. Fortu-
nately, true education is also the best possible way of knowing the world for what it is.

TEN

COLONIALISM

W HEN YOU USE THE POWER OF
Reason as strictly as you can to make judgments about the
voice of the world, some unsettling things can happen to
you. Consider the frightening results of a little experiment in
thinking that anyone can perform:

The dramatic power of the story of Jesus and the adulter-
ous woman is not great. Although the punishment she faces
is indeed lethal, her crime seems trivial. She is not a monster
of depravity. We have reached an interesting and useful understanding of that story, but is it the understanding we
might have reached if we had been able to share the supposed moral outrage of her would-be executioners? If her
crime had been truly monstrous, would we still be ready to
conclude that Jesus had brought those men out of a bad condition and into a good one?

Suppose the culprit were not merely a self-indulgent
woman, but a different sort of criminal, one who arouses in
us no sympathetic sentiment whatsoever. An Adolf Eichmann, perhaps, of whom we will *not* say that he merely
succumbed, as we all might, to a natural human weakness.
Ought Jesus to deal with his case as he did with the woman?
Will we be pleased with the end of the tale, when the accusers drop their stones and walk away, having become better? Will we still believe them bettered? And whether they
are better or not, can we still suppose that justice has been
done when this culprit is let off with nothing more than
advice?

I imagine now, that, having heard of my deliberations in
these matters, Jesus, troubled as to whether he may have set
a bad example, and hoping to do better, comes to me seeking understanding.

How shall I, from now on, he will ask, learn to find the
mark that must lie somewhere along the line that runs from
a silly and self-indulgent woman at one end to Adolf Eichmann at the other? At what point should I put aside the

business of awakening the accusers and take up instead the business *of* the accusers?

Or should I, he asks, simply withdraw, saying to the accusers: Who am I to tell you what is right? And saying that, don't I also say, Seek some *other* to tell you what is right? If that is what you would recommend, then I must point out that it is exactly what I did. To each man I said: Ask *yourself* that question, and be advised by the one authority that has no other axe to grind but yours. Is there some better authority to whom I should have sent them? Do you have some suggestions as to who that other should be?

So I explain that, in sense that goes deeper even than the customs and the laws, a "criminal" is one who does harm. I talk about harm, the various degrees of harm, and even different kinds of harm—physical harm and psychological harm; harm that lasts, and harm that goes away; harm that sometimes actually helps, and harm that never helps; harm in a good cause, and harm in a bad cause. In the original case, Jesus has himself done no harm. Indeed, he has made the accusers better than they were, and may even have done some good for the accused, beyond saving her life, although she wasn't all that bad to begin with. She hadn't really done much harm, I guess. But if the culprit were Eichmann, who did harm beyond our powers to believe, although believe it we must, then Jesus would do a terrible thing indeed, not only to turn aside his accusers, but to say thereafter, Doth no man accuse thee? Neither do I. Go, and sin no more.

At the same time, though, I know that I am also talking about that mark on the line that runs from one culprit to the other. That mark is now all the harder to find, too, for I have made it dependent on all those marks by which the various sorts of harm, which can be told from one another only by finding some other obscure marks along another line. If I am to instruct Jesus, for instance, in distinguishing between harm done in a good cause and harm done in a bad one, is he not likely to ask for some way of finding a certain mark along the line that runs from one cause to the other? And will he remind me, as Plato does, that everybody always thinks that his cause is good. No one says, Aha! I will now do some evil in a bad cause.

Is there any point, Jesus asks, sounding more and more like Socrates, in asking whether a cause is good or bad? A cause is not a person, that it can will its deeds. And if the ends do not justify the means, neither do they condemn them. No matter what the cause, bravery is bravery, and cowardice, cowardice. Can I truly judge of deeds by judging, instead, of the cause in which they were done?

His questions make me wary. Suppose, for instance, that I am so frightened by the prospect of the next great war that I insist that there can be no justification whatsoever for warfare, and that the harm it will certainly do is utterly out of proportion to the supposed and merely possible good of any "good cause" in which it might be done. Few will accuse me of irrationality for that view. But I have already put it to Jesus that there is some cause, in this case the punishment of Eichmann, in which we *must* do harm, if we are to be just. And still there are few who will accuse me of irrationality, but Jesus will be one of them.

And what of the stone-carriers, he asks, Must I do harm to them, in the name of a good cause? Before, I brought them into some goodness. Must I *now*, because the cause is great, leave them in some badness?

His questions bring me into that deep discomfort of which Socrates spoke. I am unsure of everything. I would rather not stay around to hear the argument out. I would prefer to go to a ball game. And ball games, like all their uncountable equivalents, if taken in strong enough and continual doses, provide the hope of never falling into such discomfort. I would like to wash my hands of the whole business and just live. I would like to rule my own little kingdom, and keep it simple, and not be bothered by questions that have an unsettling look of "the ultimate" about them. When the time comes to do harm, or to refrain from doing harm, well, presuming that I can control myself at all, I'll just try to figure something out. Besides, there already are all sorts of answers to such questions. You could look them up. And a fat lot of good they have done us in all these thousands of years, so that we can still bother ourselves with them. As to advising Jesus as to how to handle the Eichmann case, I'll just forget the whole business.

But, having suffered at least partial and occasional education, I find myself just as troubled by forgetting the whole business as by remembering it. I can not forget utterly that wretched Petronilla, the child who lives in me, and whose rearing seems not only my obligation, but my *natural* obligation, far stronger even than a legal or social obligation. I also have in my little kingdom a certain nagging counselor, who seems to have appointed himself Petronilla's advocate. He keeps asking questions that do *not* smell of the ultimate, and can not be dismissed out of hand as beyond my powers to answer.

He insists upon asking, Which would you say, O King, is the better parent and most likely to consider whether harm might ever be remedial, one who gives thought or one who does not give thought to the difference between Eichmann and the woman taken in adultery? What king, he asks, is the more likely to rule well in his own country, he who bothers his head as to the distinction of the good cause from the bad, or he who goes to the ball game?

Unfortunately, those questions are not at all hard to answer. Indeed, of their answers I must say that I know them, and not merely that I am informed of them.

Accordingly, I know better than to say, Listen, many have already considered such questions, and their conclusions are easily found; when I have need of them, I'll look them up, and, somehow or other, choose among them as to which is wisdom and which is not.

He would surely say, And who then, O King, would be

ruling in this little country of yours, when you choose to follow the counsel of this one or that of a host of foreign advisors?

To that I would have to answer, *I* will still be ruling, for it will be I who chooses.

And he will ask, How, O King, will you know to make that choice wisely unless you have given thoughtful consideration to some principle by which to distinguish between good causes and bad causes, which will also be a principle by which to distinguish between the better and the worse, and to distinguish among the many answers in your collection of foreign sages?

Here is a truth that most teachers will not tell you, even if they know it: Good training is a continual friend and a solace; it helps you now, and assures you of help in the future. Good education is a continual pain in the neck, and assures you always of more of the same. When training is not called forth into service, it lies quietly in its place. Neither the accountant nor the chemist nor even the tuner of engines is vexed by thoughtful doubting right in the middle of the ball game by the murmurings of his skill. But any one of them, all unmolested by an obedient training, may notice, even at the ball game, that he has not tried to understand something that he knows he *should* try to understand, and be vexed. Training is a good dog, a constant companion and an utterly loyal and devoted friend, and everyone should have one. Education is a nagging counselor. And, I am convinced, everyone *does* have one. It happens, however, that some nagging counselors have grown strong by a certain kind of nourishment. Others are weak and puny, even infantile, having never been nourished at all.

What becomes of one who is not nourished at all, and does he fare any better if he is wrongly nourished, like a child fed on cookies and pop? Who has been the counselor's parent, to make of him the worthy parent of the child who dwells in the same kingdom? If it is the counselor's job to keep the king on the right path, who is the king who keeps *him* on track?

Here in my kingdom, everyone seems to be an immigrant. And some of them seem more correctly understood not as immigrants in good faith, looking to make new lives in a new land, but as covert agents of a foreign power living in deep cover. Some of those, once I think to seek them out, are easy to spot. They are voices from the world, all the sentiments and prejudices who crossed these borders in my childhood, and will continue to arrive and find homes so long as that childhood persists in me. They are the proponents of all those learnings that we have lately come to distinguish as -isms of all kinds, who cause in me responses so automatic that I am always in danger of deciding that "automatic" is the same as "natural." For that reason, they all seem to carry licenses of authority, and some of them look so official that I seem to have appointed them a National Commission and given them the name of "conscience."

Anyone who undertakes a program of self-government must sooner or later deal with the unpleasant possibility that what culture and tradition celebrate as conscience may not in fact be the same sort of advisor as the wise and nagging counselor who asks hard questions.

What, exactly, do we mean by conscience, and, even more important, what exactly could we *choose* to mean by conscience? It is surely not a thing out there in the world, but rather a something here inside, like intelligence. It is an idea, an idea that we can work on, changing it or enlarging it, or even, as the history of anyone will sadly tell, distorting it into a remarkably convenient set of rationalizations. "Always let your conscience be your guide" is advice of doubtful value. Conscience must be, among other things, a list of sayings, an anthology of quotations and precepts. Where did they come from, and who first wrote them on my empty slate, and why? Have they been tested for sense and consistency, so that, by doing such a test for myself, I might confirm them and truly adopt them as though they were indeed the result of my own thoughtfulness? Up to now, I have adopted them only as the nightingale adopts the cuckoo; they were dropped in my nest. I imagined them "mine." They all came to me in some personal equivalent of a prehistoric age, like admonitory dreams in the long sleep of Petronilla. When I awoke, an event that I can not remember, there they were, and I could only have thought them a part of me.

If a true education is the process that makes us able to be good, and if obedience to conscience is all that we need to be good, then education is nothing more than the inculcation of the collected sayings of conscience. That inculcation will be all the more effective if those sayings are recited in the ears of sleeping children. They thus become, to every awakening child, a body of ancient lore, for there is no more distant past than the past within, beyond the reach of examination, and long, long out of mind. The unexamined sentiments, beliefs, and precepts that flavor all my thinking have been around in me forever, for this life is all the forever that I can possibly know. But they all came, in the beginning, from somewhere else. They are not natives. I have to suspect that a thoughtful examination will lead to the naturalization of some, and the deportation of others, and that the business of a true education is to be able to discover which are which.

Home Rule in one's own kingdom can not truly come from the expulsion of all foreign agents. With, perhaps, one very puzzling exception, every agent in my kingdom is a foreign agent. Each one is somebody from outside, because, except for the one somebody who is just plain me, there is no place else to come from. They can not truly be deported, however reprehensible and disruptive, for that would require nothing less than self-inflicted, seductive and deliberate amnesia. The men who didn't throw their stones did not merely disregard the law by which they took them up, and they certainly did not deport it; they annulled it. They governed that which had governed them. This is why self-government is such a tremendous undertaking, and one to whose mere beginnings a whole life might easily be devoted. It is a task thrust upon an infant king, who must rear himself and come to govern all those much older and stronger inhabitants of his land whose natural tendency is to govern the king. That it can be done in any degree at all is truly a wonder, which is why we have come to see it as nothing less than the gift of a god.

A prudent king will do all that he can to understand the inhabitants of his land. He needs somebody like a Madison, to write his own version of the tenth *Federalist Paper*, which considers the problem of factionalism in a constitutional republic. How shall government go well, when parties with opposing interests and desires are all citizens who merit representation? How will small parties be protected from the greater power of large parties, and, most important of all, what will become of the republic should some faction grow large enough to constitute a majority? If we don't trouble ourselves much with such questions anymore, it is because we usually suppose that the Constitution Madison was defending has provided the answers, but also that we suppose, quite wrongly, that "faction" is just another word for a group of people who want pretty much the same thing. But that wasn't exactly what Madison had in mind, any more than Plato, who spoke of faction as the root of all social disorder and catastrophe.

He was thinking of opinion clubs which, by the nature of their opinions, simply can not compromise. We might best see his meaning by thinking of Palestinians and Israelis, or Indians and Pakistanis, or even northern Irish and southern Irish. Between one man who claims that God says A, and another who claims that God says B, there is no road that leads to a middle ground, nor is there any hope of rational argument and demonstration that may bring the one to agree with the other. If there are disputants who are willing to kill each other over that disagreement, then they will kill each other forever, and in perfectly good conscience at that.

Such factions cause quite enough trouble out there in the world, where I can do nothing at all about them, but their internal equivalents cause just as much trouble right here in me, where I ought to be able to do something about them, and don't. What I have just said reveals a factional disagreement in my own kingdom.

I have one counselor who says, Listen, you are what you are because of powers and influences not of your choosing and beyond your control. You have to learn to live with that.

Then there is another, who says, Well, let's not quarrel as to whether you are, right here and now, the product of outside influences. Indeed, how could that be very far from the truth? But are you not also, as of now, one who *sees* that he is a product of outside influences, and has thus separated himself in some sense from them, as the seer must be separate from the seen, and has thus constituted himself an *inside* influence? Therefore, while it would be only decent and humane to excuse all your past vice and folly as utterly beyond your poor power to control, your future vice and folly will have to be seen as failings to which you contribute as an inside influence.

And to this the first responds, Bunk. That "seer" is an illusion, a rationalization. There is no self at all, but only what nature and nurture have written.

What compromise can they strike, these counselors who are also leaders of populous factions? One of them is made up of fears, and the other of hopes. They are not exactly the same as people who claim to know what God says, but they are like them in a very important way. The difference is in detail, not in principle. They can not be shown either right or wrong by Reason. They can not be converted, nor can they be ignored, for they are forever scuffling in the streets, like the Montagues and Capulets, although they will by no means be reconciled in the end. My best hope must be that they can be governed.

The understanding of philosophy that I can best fathom is the one provided by a character in one of Plato's dialogues, the *Theatatus*. It is a certain Theodorus, a genial old mathematician, who defines philosophy, without intending anything grand and complicated, as the habit of "quietly asking and answering in turn." That "quietly" is very important. Thinking is a conversation, not a confrontation, and it proceeds by argument, which is not anything like a quarrel. It is typical of factionaries, and of the factionaries in me, the dissolved beliefs and prejudices, the voices of tradition and authority, and the conclusions of my own disorderly thinking, that they are not quiet. They behave like peace marchers and gun collectors whose parades have unfortunately collided. They shout and interrupt. They "ask" only in some peculiar sense, for their asking is a challenge rather than a search for understanding. To their questions, they do not truly expect new answers. And they "answer" not by walking along the line of the question, but by breaking it. They do not wait their turns, but interrupt whenever they feel like it, for *feeling* is to them the great enabling principle that justice would be in the well-governed self.

I once paid attention to a priest who was being interviewed on television. He was asked whether he *himself* was willing to "condemn" the violent tactics of the IRA. His answer was remarkable:

How can we, he said, bring ourselves to condemn the violence of a few individuals unless we first condemn the official and much greater violence of mighty nations? How can we call "evil" the terrorism of some men, until we have denounced as evil the hideous and inhuman terrorism of the arms race, far more threatening than the bombs of the IRA?

He spoke solemnly and sincerely, a deep pain in his look. His questioner was satisfied. He paused a long moment, reverently, and went on to talk about the St. Patrick's Day Parade. The discussion was over.

I wondered a lot about that priest's inner kingdom. What voices were shouting in him, and which had fallen silent? Where was his nagging counselor, or for that matter, the official nagging counselor of his persuasion—Aquinas, who held that there was only one Reason, and that it pertained to all that we could know? Mine, had I made such an answer, would at least have asked me about the strange fact that when asked what judgment *I* had made, I answered by talking about some judgment that *we* could not make, as though I were somehow licensed to speak for every person in the world. Most of all, my counselor would ask some reconsideration of my truly astonishing contradiction. I can easily imagine the conversation that would follow, the quietly asking and answering in turn for which television does not have time.

You have just said, have you not, that *anyone* who would condemn the violent tactics of a few individuals would first have to pass a test, a test that would require some prior condemnation of other violent tactics?

Well, yes, that is what I have said.

Did you also intend to give the impression that you yourself had already passed that test, that you were indeed ready to condemn what you describe as the greater evil? Or are you disqualifying yourself as one who would condemn the lesser because you have *not* condemned the greater?

I must admit, nay, affirm, that I have condemned the greater evil, and I can hardly imagine how Reason might demonstrate me wrong in doing that.

So you have passed the test. Why don't you just go ahead and condemn that "lesser evil"?

What can I say to that, except to admit that I hadn't been making sense. So my questioner would want to consider further the possibility that I had been irrational not by oversight, but because certain voices in me were shouting.

In itself the irrationality was quite outrageous, but all the more so because it was committed in what seemed a studied pretense of rationality. It was worded *as though* it were logic. You ask me if I can say Y? Well, *no one* can say Y without having said X. I do, of course, say X, but I will still not say Y, thus suggesting that saying Y is not enough to bring me to say X, and revealing that something else must be necessary for the saying of X, and that the relationship between X and Y is not quite as direct and "logical" as I have implied. But it did *sound* logical, didn't it? What was the need of such pretense? What factions required it?

Orwell provided us a memorable understanding in saying that the strange language of government grew out of the need of government continually to "defend the indefensible." That makes us comfortable, because "government" is somebody else, and we think ourselves unindicted by Orwell's fine phrase. But I too am government. Whatever nonsense I may talk comes straight from my throne. It is an enunciation of nothing less than "policy," some internal principle by which I work, and which dictates not only my deeds, but my thoughts and my words, which are also deeds.

My counselor would surely ask me just *who* is making the policy in this little kingdom. Is it one certain brand of Irishness, perhaps? Can it be Catholicism? Is it some homegrown version of the one or the other, some private misunderstanding of special ethnic or religious beliefs, traditions and customs? Is it perhaps much simpler? Some desire to make friends and influence people, or some fear of offending certain people? Surely, in a mind that *can* take the grasp of itself, such an astonishing, and apparently deliberate, crime against your own mind must rise from somewhere deep in the belly, from the demanding voices of those who do not quietly ask and answer in turn, but shout, and will neither ask nor answer, but only proclaim.

ELEVEN

The
WORLD
of
NO ONE
At
ALL

F EARS SHOUT EVEN LOUDER
than appetites. In one way, it is good for us that fear blots
out thought and turns us into its robots. In emergencies,
nothing is more useful than utterly unthinking fear, which
turns on automatic and instantaneous responses, and the
person in whom acute fear does not have that effect will not
last long on the roads. But fear does not limit itself to imme-
diate physical emergencies, and imagination easily provides
it nourishment by picturing an endless anthology of all the
bad things that can happen to us, as well as those that surely
will happen to us. Even in quiet reflection, fear scrambles
thought.

So it is that we are inclined to reject as simply preposterous a notion of Epictetus which holds that nothing bad
can happen to a good person. We have plenty of evidence to
the contrary, ranging from flat tires and toothaches at one
end of the scale to death and destruction at the other.

Toothaches and flat tires some of us may actually escape,
but not death and destruction. Death and destruction, however, which are the natural destinies of all creatures and
things, are not the killers and destroyers, and it is a strange
understanding of the world by which we think the former as
"bad" as the latter. Stranger still, we actually take comfort
from believing that, since we are regularly victims of what
we call bad, then we must be the good, and the innocent. To
be stricken with a lethal disease, therefore, is to be perse-
cuted by an implacable and irresistible tyrant, and the suf-
ferer wins not only sympathy, but moral approbation, as the
aggrieved party in an unfair proceeding. He seems, all guilt-
less, to have been condemned. Therefore, he must be the
just party to this transaction. That a "bad thing" has happened to him, proves him one of the "good people." It is as
though sickness and every other condition of suffering were
a vast prison, in which every single prisoner has been given a
bum rap, unjustly accused, unlawfully convicted, and sen-
tenced to death.

163

In what passes for an age of pragmatic materialism, that is a remarkably superstitious view of the natural world. There is no "progress" in the mind that moves from the belief that the trees and rivers have certain intentions, to the belief that viruses and molecules have intentions. Nor is that mind any the better for admitting, as most will, that it "knows," of course, that a virus has no intention, but that it nevertheless still *feels* as though that were so. That's what the belly says.

Epictetus was doing no more than reaffirming, simply and literally, a very old idea. He could see no sense at all in presuming the existence of goodness or badness where there was no intention, no will. He knew that people fell sick and died, and that they maimed and killed each other routinely, either in the name of the Law or out of it. He was not a childish dreamer who imagined that the "good," if only they believed something or other with all their hearts, would somehow be magically protected from the natural processes in the world and in themselves. He knew, and anyone can, through nothing more than a little reflection, that it comes to pass with the good exactly as it comes to pass with the bad. Chance and the world happen to them all. And it is the same, whether we imagine that the world includes inordinately touchy gods who take revenge for affront, or implacable diseases lying in wait for those who don't eat enough fiber.

But I suspect that for Epictetus the question was not how to escape the gods or the diseases; it was rather, how to remain a good person when stricken by either, as we all must be in one way or another. To be sick, or to suffer, is inevitable; but to become bitter and vindictive in sickness and suffering, and to surrender to irrationality, supposing yourself the innocent and virtuous victim of the evil intentions of the world, is not inevitable. The appropriate answer to the question, Why me? is the other question, Why not me? Those who can ask the first, must have already devised some answer to the second, however unconsciously and incoher-

ently. It is the most important implication of Epictetus'
strange assertion that a good person would know better than
to devise that answer, an answer that would have to be irrational, setting the deviser above or beyond the natural order
in which life takes place.

The curious proposition of Epictetus can be easily understood in the simplest of examples. I find myself once again in
the tollbooth line, the shortest one, into which I have auda-
ciously and cunningly found my way, and actually escaped,
this time, serious injury or even death, while also, this time,
failing to visit either on other drivers. I am, of course, going
somewhere. My mission, unlike that of the woman ahead of
me, is important. Much, much will depend on my timely
arrival at my important destination, where those who await
me will be able to do nothing, nothing at all, without me. I
have already asked the usual question, Why me? Now I am
busy trying to provide a convincing answer to the neat question, Why not me? I have made and accepted my own version of the natural order of things, and actually supposed a
universe that has, or damn well ought to have, my convenience in mind. And there she sits, pawing, all in vain,
through eighteen pounds of purse. Harm is being done. Notice that I have cleverly put this in the passive, a traditional
and convenient way of suggesting that there can be a deed
without a doer, and harm without a harmer.

But harm, real harm, truly *is* done; a badness has been
brought into being. And there *is* an agent of harm; a person
who could choose either to do it or not, has done it. I am the
agent. There is no other possible agent in sight. The change-
less woman is, in this case, as utterly without intentions as
the rain that might fall before I reach that stupendously important destination. Should that happen, will I blame the
rain, and fume at the Great Order of Things, which is obviously against me? In this context, of course, such a reaction seems preposterous, even ludicrous, in fact, hardly to be
believed. But an honest inventory of the past compels me to

notice that I have, quite contrary to what seems just now nothing but simple good sense, occasionally done such a thing. Others have, too, I think. How strange.

The event, perhaps, is trivial; the condition it brings is not. It is supremely important. It is a temporary destruction of a person, and, for all I know, a harbinger of a permanent destruction, a lifelong absence of self-rule. (Can such a condition be possible?) If I fail to take it seriously *because* of the supposed triviality of the event, which I have already taken seriously enough to bring about my own derangement, Epictetus will surely ask me how I intend to measure events, so that I will know which are worth the effort of self-rule, and which may be shrugged off as no big deal. He will also ask me exactly how I intend to instruct Petronilla in this matter, so that she too, like me, will be perfectly capable of thoughtful self-government in the great matters but practical enough not to waste her mental energies on the small. My answers would be, well, certainly entertaining, provided, of course that I made any at all, which would depend on whether I judged the questions themselves a great matter or no big deal. If I am truly to answer Epictetus, and not simply to declaim against him, I can answer only in Reason, only in reasonable conversation, in rationally measurable sayings, in quietly asking and answering in turn.

There is no secret in the art of distinguishing between the better and the worse. The consideration of the questions of goodness and badness is no more mysterious than the consideration of the square of the hypotenuse. Talking about Goodness, the crime that Socrates promised to commit every day, requires no faculty that you and I do not possess by Nature. It requires no special knowledge that only a special few can claim, and no official licensing. It depends not at all on the authority of others, who are all nothing more, or less, than other parties to the conversation, and all of whose sayings are subject to the same rational testing as ours, and whose worth is not in the mouth that utters them, but in

that mind that can test them. Nor is the rational consideration of questions of goodness and badness dependent in any
way upon feelings, except insofar as such a consideration
may be impossible in the presence of certain feelings, as my
self-government at the tollbooth is impossible because of
what is not only a feeling, but equally a desire to have that
feeling—a not uncommon perversity.

That perversity seems to me one of the great mysteries of
human behavior. Why is it that I can so often discover, in
looking carefully at what I have done, that I have clearly
wanted to be irrational? Especially in anger or desperation, I
can see, by stepping back only a little way from the "front"
of myself, the public display, that I have found in deeds and
events exactly the excuse I was looking for to put on a display of anger or desperation. Evidence, both the evidence of
the daily world, and, even more conclusively, the evidence
of thoughtful literature, suggests that this perversity is not
unique to me. It is, indeed, general. That fact has often been
taken to support the convenient belief that "man" is, deep
down where it really counts, an irrational creature, whose
momentary outbursts of rationality are aberrations from the
normal. It is another face of the belief that Socrates is a freak,
a marvelous and admirable freak, but a freak nevertheless.
Those who take that view, whether through serious thought
of their own or merely because they have often heard it said,
are naturally scornful of those who believe, or seem to believe, in the "perfectibility of man." Between the two parties, there is incessant disagreement, and their quarrel
certainly has about it the look of either/or, so that those who
have joined neither party are nagged by the thought that
they will eventually, if they want to understand how it is
with us, have to take one side or the other. That is bunk. It is
a quarrel, on both sides, made entirely of worthless statements in the World of We All.

There is no such reality as "how it is with *us*," any more
than there is some reality in which "we" have given up slav-

ery. Must I conclude, fuming in the tollbooth line, whether man—or, in this case, woman—is truly a rational creature, who might someday reach the perfection of a truly rational life? "Man" is just a tricky way of saying we. It is not my job either to make man perfectly rational or to figure out whether that can ever be done. It is my job to *be* rational, and I have no doubt at all that I have that power—sometimes. I am not appointed to decide, for now and for always, whether the omniscience of God, if there is such a thing, is an absolute impediment to the free will of man, if there is such a thing. If I set aside the task of my own self-government until that happy day when "man" shall have learned it, I will continue to do harm for quite a long time. I will also continue to imagine that the world is a place in which bad things, great and small, befall good and innocent people— especially me.

The sense of persecution, or of just plain bad luck, that many people carry through life is really a twisted testimony to their inklings of rationality. He who supposes that the deck is stacked, must begin by supposing that there is a deck, an order of things, and one that can actually be either a right order or a wrong order. By "wrong" and "right," to be sure, he means wrong or right *for him*, by which he also means, usually, wrong or right for the fulfillment of his desires or the alleviation of his fears.

Nevertheless, he is right in principle. There is a deck, and it is stacked. But decks don't stack themselves. It takes a cheater to do that, and there is no cheater in the natural order of things, a fact that is demonstrated not merely by the findings of science but simply by the *possibility* of science, which could not exist at all if someone were able to fool around with Mother Nature. If the complainer's deck is stacked, some *person* has stacked it. It is because I have stacked my own deck, making trumps of all my desires, that I do not notice the irrationality of my expectation that the tollbooth lanes will open at my coming. Like just about anyone else, I *want* my road open. When I find it closed, whether by a woman without exact change, or by sickness and the threat of death itself, what I find is perfectly natural, and neither bad nor good. It is what I do to myself in such adversities that can be either bad or good.

There is another, and better, way to think about what I have called the World of No One at All. It was also known, in earlier times, as Necessity. Ancient thinkers did indeed mean by that term some of what we mean, all that is summed up in our recognition of the fact that we do have to eat and sleep. But they seem to have meant something more, the fact that the world does have to be the world that it is, that all things are subject to principles, by which they are what they are, and by which they also become, inevitably, what they become. In that understanding, there is no possibility of escape from Necessity, of course, but, even more important, there is no *good* to be taken or supposed in the escape from Necessity. Far from it, for the dream of escape from Necessity, of special dispensation from the order of the world, is a lie about the world. When I fume in the tollbooth line, I am not a good person to whom a bad thing is happening. I am a liar who is getting what he deserves.

Many pages ago, I made a dismal list of many, but surely not all, of the "bad" things that will surely happen to Petronilla, and, given only enough life, to any child. It was not out of some especially gloomy cast of mind that I chose those disasters, but only out of common knowledge. And out of the same, I could equally have made a very cheerful list of "good" things that will befall, given only enough life, the child whose rearing has fallen to me, and any child. While chance may share them out in varying measures, all of those conditions are, like eating and sleeping, nothing but Necessity. They are not exactly "what happens" in the world, for the world knows neither joy nor grief, but they are what happens in persons *because* of what happens in the world.

I do not have the power to see to it that no harm or un-happiness befalls Petronilla. Neither do I have, as Saint Peter is said to have had, the power to put her to sleep. She will have to live in the world, and take what comes. In misery, what will she do to herself? Will she add to her misery the injury of making herself bitter or vindictive? Will she com-pound disappointment and loss with vain imaginings, sup-posing the world her foe, and mistaking her desires and appetites for the justice which has been denied her? Or will she—and this is the true alternative to all those unhappy possibilities—learn to make sense?

Sense can be made. Indeed, it must be made, and made by a person, for it does not simply appear in the world. With the making of sense in mind, it may be that one of the most important powers that I can nourish in any Petronilla is the power of language, and the habit of thoughtful attention to language. Consider my wily passive at the tollbooth. It is a way of speaking that allows me to think what I *want* to think. Another way of speaking would show me that I am thinking nonsense. If I had used an active verb, saying that somebody *is doing* harm, I would have seen at once the need for identifying that somebody. And I would have been led to myself. That habitual passive now seems remarkably conve-nient for those times in which I prefer not to understand.

There are also many words that we customarily use for that very purpose—the prevention of understanding. If I think myself the victim of persecution, I have made an invis-ible passive. Any sensible person would ask me, Just who is it who persecutes you? Where there is persecution, which argues the existence of intention and will, there must be a persecutor. Where there is oppression or deprivation, there must be an oppressor or a depriver. Where such agents are not to be found, there it must be the case that I am *not* perse-cuted, oppressed, or deprived, but something else. What is that something else? Is it mere Necessity? Is it something that I myself am doing, all unwittingly?

But, while such thinking might prevent me from being a fool, it does not have to make me a simpleton. I have, and I think everyone has, incontrovertible evidence that some persons do sometimes persecute, deprive, and oppress. Where is such evidence found? While I may have my suspicions of other persons, of course, simple reasoning requires me to admit that I can not *know* the wills and intentions of others, but only speculate about them. They are not *in* my experience, as my own will and intention would be, if only I would consider them carefully. The incontrovertible evidence that I do have, therefore, comes from my knowledge that *I* sometimes persecute, deprive, and oppress, combined with what seems a fairly safe belief that I can hardly be the *only* person on the face of Earth who does such things. Some others may do likewise. But who, exactly? And why?

I don't mean to answer those questions. They can be answered only in particular cases. But if Petronilla had the inclination and power to *ask* those questions in particular cases, the answers might be very useful both for the health of her mind and the alleviation of needless misery. And should the questions prove unanswerable, that fact itself brings some new realization into her mind. When she can not answer them, she *can* say—privately, thank goodness— Maybe I am not making sense when I talk to myself.

Thinking is talking to oneself. I can not think outside of my mind, or in anything other than my mind. The mind's work in thinking is a continual conversation, an asking and answering, which is why it is a good idea to talk to yourself as much as possible. If you'd rather not do it aloud, you might at least try to move your lips. The same is true of reading. There is no advantage to be taken from reading or thinking quickly, and often much harm. We are, after all, bodies, and it is, in spite of some suggestions in Plato, not easy to conclude that we can ever know anything that didn't first come to us in the flesh, in experience. Words and statements have a puzzling double life; they must live in the mouth before they can live in the mind. Thus it is that our own thinking has a puzzling double life.

There is in thinking a quality that I do not mean to call "sexual," but which nevertheless seems very like the process of sexual reproduction. From the point of view of the species, if a species could have a point of view, the great advantage of sexual reproduction is the endless variety of possibilities to which it leads. Every creature born of sex is absolutely new and unique. Our thinking, on the other hand, is often amoebic, born only of itself. If it is to be continually renewed, it needs new seed. If we think only the thoughts that are customary to us, and listen only to the words of those who are "of our mind," we are little likely to find refreshment and renewal in our minds, and thus all too likely to suppose that we have come to the end of all deliberations that we have to make.

Although it often seems that some people live entirely by accident or at whim, following now this influence or that appetite, it is simply not possible to live a random or disorderly life any more than water can run downhill by any but the shortest path. That random, "blindly floundering" life out of which Prometheus led us is simply the life of unknowing animals. Now that we are minded animals, our floundering has a different quality. There is always *some* order, some principle at work in all human deeds, and some new seed of thought being sown in us whether we know it or not. Should the governing principle of one's life be the satisfaction of desire, or the service of some belief, the result is the same—a governed life, to be sure, but a life whose governor does not live in the kingdom he governs. Anybody at all can engender thought in me by whetting my appetite, and arousing not only my habitual desires, but also novel desires, and all the more alluring for their novelty.

Many can bring me into or out of this or that belief. Like everyone else—I might better say, like every other child—I know what I want, and I believe what I believe. What I do not always know is whether I *should* want what I want, and whether what I believe makes sense. And into that condition I must fall unless I have some understanding of what I might mean by my "knowing." If I am stuck in that condition, not even knowing that I am stuck in that condition, then my fervent partisanship in any company of belief whatsoever is not, as I might well pronounce it, a Great Affirmation of Meaning and Purpose. It is no less an accident of history than my blood type, and has no more meaning or purpose than my social security number. Thus, in the search for new seed, Christians should listen for a while to Marx or Hume, and Marxists should spend some time with Thomas à Kempis or Marcus Aurelius.

But Petronilla, who is my child and me at the same time, is not, and should not be, either a Christian or a Marxist, or any other kind of -ist. She is a child. To be an -ist of any sort may be suitable to a mind that has already taken the grasp of itself and reached the determinations of Reason possible to such a mind, but I suspect that such a mind is not likely to find an acceptable -ism. Jesus himself, in the story of the would-be stone-throwers, led those men both to lead and to follow not an -ism, but themselves. He called forth in them the willing of grown-ups, not the willingness of a child.

His words were to them the seed of a new birth of thought, and the parent of any child is put by nature in the role that Jesus plays in that story. I do not mean to suggest by that, or depend on, any religious belief, but only nature. Parent is parent, and child is child. They are given to each other in a perfectly natural process, and that perfectly natural process has an analog in a larger but equally natural process, the provision of the seed of thought.

This is the great value of literacy, that by its power our parents long dead can speak to us, and we can listen to them. And if they do not seem to answer when we ask, it may be only because we have not turned the page. And this is the great value of a thoughtful parent, or any other true teacher in any other guise—that he has turned many pages.

When my Petronilla, or the Petronilla in me, is *truly* oppressed, truly the victim of a person's ill will, I will at least be able to offer to her consideration, if I have turned the pages and listened, what some of my many parents have offered to mine. How better could I begin, for instance than by telling her, in whatever terms best suit her condition, what Marcus Aurelius had to say? "When anyone does you a wrong, set yourself at once to consider what was the point of view, good or bad, that led him wrong. As soon as you perceive it, you will be sorry for him, not surprised or angry."

If I had leaned out the window and shouted obscenities at the woman in the tollbooth line, which of us would *surely* have already been made a worse person, and which would still have some chance of avoiding that badness? Which of us is pitiable? Which of us stands in greater need of some help, of some wise parent, of some occasion of education? Such questions are not at all too hard for a child to consider. Of that, too, I have incontrovertible proof, the hard evidence of experience, for I am the child in the tollbooth line who now considers them.

TWELVE

HOW
to
LIVE
(I Think)

I HAVE HABITUALLY IMAGINED —"guessed" might be the more honest word—that Reason is high, very high, a lofty and distant realm where "matters of the greatest import" dwell, and where mighty minds move among them. And accordingly, I have supposed Unreason, a complete irrationality, as low as Reason is high, the very pit, the abyss, the frozen floor of hell. I tend to populate the two realms, therefore, with the extremest of cases, Socrates and Jesus above, and Hitler and Jack the Ripper below. Thus, while intending to distinguish the former from the latter, I end up making them all alike in one supremely important respect. I set Socrates and Hitler both beyond my grasp, far, far away from me, and console myself for being unable to sit with the former by supposing that I am, and by virtue of the same limitations, in no danger of joining the ranks of the latter. It is all bunk. I can easily do either. Or both. That I seldom realize that is testimony to the fact that I have habitually mistaken schooling for education. The idea that careful and attentive rationality can be achieved only by those who have taken the right courses is profitable for schools.

No mind can be more rational, or more irrational, than another. One mind can be more or less often more rational, or irrational than another. In my occasional lucid moments, I have as much light as Socrates, and in Unreason, I am as benighted as Hitler. In certain moments, it is only by humanity's good luck that I am not empowered to direct the destinies of nations, and in others, that may be a pity. And the same is true of you, and of each of us. Reason and Unreason are never far away from any mind. They are neither far above us nor far beneath us. It is one and the same thing to be rational in considering the beginning and the end of all things, and to be rational in telling yourself how to behave in the supermarket checkout line, which might even be the more difficult task, the more likely to be influenced by strong feelings and desires. There is surely a difference between a man who would slaughter millions for the sake of his appetites and beliefs, and a man who turns, however briefly, into a monster of rage when a woman driver turns out not to have exact change in the exact change lane, but it is not a difference in degrees of rationality.

The clearest and most honest assessment of my own life that I have been able to make seems to suggest that I am not called to undertake the great consideration of the beginning and end of all things, the one consideration by which, in the opinion of Aquinas, a person might be accounted truly wise. It is not for me. On the other hand, I am not so situated in this life that I will have to prevent myself, by a scrupulous and rational examination of my appetites and beliefs, from bringing about the slaughter of millions in an evil cause that I can not understand as evil.

But that same assessment makes it pretty clear that I *am* called to rear Petronilla, and any child that is mine, inwardly or outwardly. And I *am* so situated in this life that I *will* have to prevent myself, by that same scrupulous and rational examination of my appetites and beliefs, from bringing about the slaughter of a human being in the exact change line, leaving in his place only a monster of Unreason. Slaughter is slaughter. In a purely material sense, of course, my act of slaughter is different from Hitler's or Jack the Ripper's, for it leaves no corpses, and the victim may—this time—live again in reasonable self-government. But in principle, it is the same act: the destruction of a person in obedience to desire unchecked by Reason. Against that charge, I would make what seems a lame and ludicrous defense by pointing out that, after all, I *have* refrained from the slaughter of millions. If I have, it may be just by luck, and proves no special virtue or restraint in me. Whatever other punishment my deed might merit, it would surely be enough for any sane and thoughtful judge to pronounce me an unfit parent of any Petronilla, and one who could not possibly provide her a true education.

Here is another definition of education that we might choose to adopt. I have to take, again, a little page from Epictetus, who was convinced that any human being has what it takes to distinguish the better from the worse, and needs only some instruction in *using* what it takes. One of the ways in which he used to make the case for that opinion was in saying something like this:

Look around you, near and far, and find someone whom you can praise, and that without any consideration of self-interest or the profit that you might take from your praising. Whom do you find to praise? The just or the unjust? The patient or the impatient? The courageous or the cowardly? Those who are owned and operated by their appetites, or those who can govern themselves and their appetites? And ask yourself, Whom do I know, or know of, who is a better person than I? And not just a better surgeon or mechanic or cook, than I, but a better *person*? What makes that one the better? What is it in me, or what lack, therefore, that makes me the worse? Is the better one the more temperate or the less temperate? More moderate, or less? More, or less, given to thoughtful consideration, and to quietly asking and answering in turn?

I have elaborated outrageously on what Epictetus actually said, but I think he would not accuse me of falsifying his intent. And his intent was simply to demonstrate a perfectly natural propensity to distinguish between the better and the worse, a propensity that works in us even when we do not take thought consciously and deliberately to make that distinction. But he was not a childish dreamer. While he did take that propensity to be nothing less than natural to us all, he was not deluded as to our powers to distort the natural in us. "There are certain things," he said, "which men who are *not altogether perverted* see by the common notions which all possess." The italics are mine.

I know some people, and I'm sure you do too, to whom I would rather not put the question of Epictetus: Whom would you praise, and why? Since I do not move in the appropriate circles, I probably do not know anyone who would choose to praise Jack the Ripper for being consistent in purpose and very good at his work, or anyone who would praise Hitler for being an astonishingly skillful and powerful politician, but I do know people who would choose to praise certain others for exactly those reasons, as though particulars were more important than principles. And I know many more who would think that by "praise" I meant also "admire" or "envy," or even "adulate" and "emulate," seeing no particular or pressing reason to distinguish among those mental deeds. I even know some, including myself, who would praise me for the skillful audacity by which I manage so often to get into the shortest line at the tollbooth.

While I can not deny my suspicion that the "altogether perverted" do indeed exist and move among us, I do not suspect that such interesting answers are always signs of the altogether perverted. They are, often, merely the answers of fashion and trend, the answers of posers. And those who pose in this context will often find themselves, unlike the altogether perverted, utterly unable to pose—unable even to *want* to pose—in the presence of the truly praiseworthy. Even in our popular literature, seen mostly these days in motion pictures or in television, goodness is celebrated. Whether in war, or sport, or business, or in the smallest enterprises of ordinary life, the appearance of steadfastness, courage, loyalty, temperance, and of the bright dawning of self-knowledge, can make even the thoughtless rejoice, however they know not why. We imagine ourselves relativists, and think ourselves sophisticated and modern to suppose that virtue depends on fashion, but even third-rate hack writers in Burbank know better.

The Great Hitler War is now far behind us, and the children among us now know surprisingly little about what we considered an epoch of monumental importance, and even a true display of the difference between Good and Evil. Now, we watch in our homes retrospective documentaries, fuzzy film clips of what has already become ancient history. There are the brave young men, standing by their fighter planes, their uniform caps appropriately askew, their arms around each others' shoulders, smiling and waving at the camera. Into the gray sky behind them, soon they will fly and disappear, some forever. They go bravely and willingly, and heavily armed, but not heavily enough, by the conviction that they choose to fight and die out of exactly the power that Socrates understood as the goal of true education—the ability to distinguish between the better and the worse.

I imagine my grandchildren's grandchildren watching the same old films. Will they be able to distinguish at once, as I can, between the brave and virtuous, doomed young men in one set of uniforms, and the deluded slaves of Unreason in the other? Will they perhaps be able to see, better than I, that persons can be good in a bad cause, and bad in a good one? Or will the struggle of causes in whose shadow *they* live lead them to imagine that goodness and badness can be acquired out there in the world by anyone who will attach himself to the right cause and fight against the wrong one?

Consider the "great causes" in which we now bring, and threaten to bring, not merely death and destruction upon each other, which will surely come anyway, but deliberate and untimely death and destruction, thus cutting off forever in millions of persons not merely goodness itself, but the very possibility of goodness. Consider all the causes in which persons can justify themselves in tremendous and appalling acts of violence and coercion, acts that they themselves, unless altogether perverted, would find unspeakably vile if committed by a single person for nothing more than his own reasons, justified by nothing more than his own beliefs, and for the gratification of nothing more than his own appetites. Such causes tend to come in pairs. Just now, there are communists and Christians, and communists of a different stripe, and Christians of a different stripe. There are fundamentalist Israelis and fundamentalist Moslems, and antifundamentalist Israelis and antifundamentalist Moslems. There are black and white, and even dark brown and light brown. There are Protestant Irish and Roman Catholic Irish. There are Indians and Sikhs. There is no counting them all.

We generally imagine great warring parties as utterly opposed to one another, true opposites, and even, for those who are members of either party, Children of Light and Children of Darkness. But the proper work of intelligence is to discover how things similar to each other are also unlike each other, and how things unlike are also alike. And it takes only a small, deliberate act of intelligence, and certainly not a high I.Q., to notice that all such great, implacable enemies have one important attribute in common. They all depend, at bottom, on some belief, some sentiment, some table of delivered precepts, or some idea of what the real world really is, which is simply not testable by Reason, not demonstrable by logic.

I imagine some great convocation on neutral ground, to which every such cause sends a representative. Just for the day, they check their bombs and guns at the door, and sit at an enormous round table to discuss, not compromise and peace, for their certainties forbid both, but survival. No such cause ever wants to go out of business. What is it, they ask themselves, that they *do* share? What great need have they in common, the very food on which they feed and grow fat? If they could somehow engender just one attribute in every person living on the face of Earth, what one attribute would serve them all equally well? What else could it be but irrationality, the condition in which we imagine that we can know the unknowable, in which we act on the orders of the belly and under the authority of the untestable dictates of belief, and by whose strength we can bestow upon credulousness the rank of virtue? What better and more faithful followers can there be than children, governed by their desires and unmindful of their minds? Every great cause in which we hate and kill persons whom we do not even know, and injure ourselves whom we also do not know, is a Children's Crusade.

But my metaphor of the great convocation of warring parties is not truly apt. There is no club of arch-villains out there in the world, whose aim is to seize my mind for evil purposes, and who would, if they could, release the virus of Unreason upon all the world. Each warring party, to be sure, does sometimes—perhaps often—presume such conscious and deliberate ill will in each and every member of the opposite warring party, but, in every case, any disinterested third party can see, on both sides, nothing but true believers, sadly sincere. In a famous phrase, which ought not to be restricted only to certain religious persuasions, a nonpartisan can easily detect the deceivers and the deceived, and also the supremely important fact that they are one and the same. No one, except a practicing criminal, or anyone altogether perverted, is truly out to trick me into believing that which he himself does not believe, or suppose that he believes, if such a distinction is possible. If I am to be tricked into believing what can not be known or affirmed by Reason, I must perform the trick for myself. Thus it is that an important benefit of the mind's grasp of itself is the power to make for oneself some coherent idea about the meaning of the word "knowledge."

If you will please read that last sentence again, you will find it, I hope, pale and puny. Neither stirring nor unsettling. Just the sort of insipid, dull, pussy-footing talk you would expect in an academic. Cowardly, in fact, for it is so impersonally phrased that no one, that is to say, no *person*, is likely to demur or demand justification. There is great danger in such a way of talking, which you will surely recognize as the language of the Land of No One at All. It permits me, or anyone, to speak what is meant to pass for "truth" without taking responsibility for my words.

So let me now put that idea in another way, moving into the world of a real person: If *you* do not know what *you* mean by the word knowledge, your mind is in disorder, and you will be an easy victim of any suggestion, accidental or designed, that seems to promise, whether you are conscious of it or not, the satisfaction of some appetite. If you happen to want the moon, or anything at all that is simply not to be had in the natural order of things, and if you happen to have no way of certainly knowing that some object of your desire is not in the natural order of things, then you will be an easy mark for all promisers of the moon, and you will often be miserable. To all other miseries, you will add the misery of believing that "bad things," like being deprived of the moon, are always happening to "good people"—you.

I am not leading up to some definition of knowledge. This is not an exercise in problem-solving. To the question, What is knowing? there is no answer, but only the continual business of answering. But in this case, as in all true thoughtfulness, *any* answering at all is better than none. Since, in understanding something, the worst possible condition is never even thinking about it at all, any thinking at all will bring a better condition, and provide the necessary step toward an even better one than that. Here is one person to whom it has never occurred to wonder what he means by knowing, and whether it is the same as believing, or imagining or supposing, or to ask whether there is some clearly identifiable difference between evidence and testimony, or whether certain things might be unknowable. And here is another person to whom it *has* occurred to wonder about such things. Which is in better condition? Which would you rather have for a parent, if you happened to be Petronilla? And here are two more people, to both of whom it has occurred to wonder. One of them, now curious about knowing, asks me what it really means to *know*, and I tell him what *I* think, and he goes away content. The other, having overheard my answer, says, Well, that may give me something to think about, but I still wonder. Which of them is in the better condition?

Of those two, it can also be said that one of them must suppose Reason lofty and remote, an esoteric power best left to the experts. The other finds it near at hand. Perform, now, a little experiment in thought with those two people. Consider again the question of Epictetus, Whom do you choose to praise? And recall the interesting idea that lies behind his question, the opinion that all persons are equipped, by the very nature that makes them persons, with the ability to tell the better from the worse. Which of the two, then, would you praise, and why? Be specific. If this were school, you would have a blue book to write your answer in. You would have to do it. But this is not school, and you don't have to answer. So ask yourself another question: Whom would you praise, one who chose not to answer, or one who answered? Would you have to guess which one to praise, or would you know which one to praise? And, having answered all those questions, what would you have to say about the strange opinion of Epictetus, which runs quite contrary to all of our popular beliefs about the transience and relativity of all ideas of better and worse?

And what have you to say about yourself? Has Epictetus described you correctly, as one who, being not altogether perverted, can see certain things by the common notions that all persons have?

After about half a century of life, and having already written almost every great work for which we remember him, Tolstoy decided that he was living to no important purpose, and that he would change himself. Thomas Aquinas, shortly before his death, although he did not know that he was soon to die, decided to write no more, saying that everything he had written was nothing but straw. What moved those tremendously accomplished men to such drastic action, I can not know, but I am willing to characterize such deeds in a perhaps uncustomary way. I would, for the sake of doing some thinking, call them artistic, and even literary. It was out of a curious mixture of self-deception and truth that Macbeth could call "life" a tale told by an idiot, full of sound and fury, and signifying nothing. That was true of *his* life, for the teller of his tale was indeed an idiot, a mindless power, compounded of an utterly irrational company of appetites, beliefs, and feelings. But to us, it seems very unlikely that such lives as those of Aquinas and Tolstoy were being told by idiots. Those men, however, seem to have decided something like that. They said, in effect, The teller of my tale has been wrong. I will take charge of this work, and make it better. I will compose the harmony that the natural order of things will not provide, and find the theme according to which all the possible contents and deeds of this life will be measured, and chosen or rejected.

That is exactly the work we call "art." It is to make of life as it comes, always at random and at the will of others, an artifact, the result of intention and design, both informed by the power to distinguish the better from the worse. It is to make of the inner life something other, and better, than the routine product of the outer life. It is to make literature, to tell a tale that makes sense, because it is told not by an idiot but by a governing mind. If Aquinas and Tolstoy seem to us to have stood in but little need of such a resurgence of mind, it may well be because they had learned more than we about idiocy and could see it even in its subtlest manifestations, where we have come to see only its grossest. Each of them said to himself, on a certain day, that his education might now begin, that some sleeping child in him could now be awakened.

It does us all significant credit that we make jokes about the search for the meaning and purpose of life, and find it most suitable for sophomore beer-busts. Epictetus would be delighted to know that, for he would find it yet another confirmation of his opinion that in our very nature there is some permanent spring of good sense. But the phrase itself, like Macbeth's maudlin effusion, points only to a world that can not be, a world where there is "life," a nonentity, a non-being. There is no life. There are living creatures. Without them, life would not persist, waiting quietly in some corner of the universe for something to inhabit. Meaning and purpose, if they appear, can appear only at the call of a living, and willing, person.

I'm pretty sure that Tolstoy and Aquinas, on their critical days of decision, were not interested in the meaning and purpose of life. They were rather interested in the meaning and purpose of the one life to which they could *give* meaning and purpose, no matter what the world might do to those lives.

There is a strange quality in religiousness. In the greatest of the "religious thinkers"—why do those quotation marks seem right?—we can always find, again and again, ideas and understandings about persons and self-knowledge that they all share, not only with each other, but with such as Epictetus and Socrates, and countless others far outside of the religious traditions of the West. But in the less than great, who are numerous, and especially in the meager of mind, who are countless, there is an admonitory and truculent concern primarily for the virtue of *other* people. If such as Thomas à Kempis and Bernard of Clairvaux are generous providers of the occasion of education, rather than reciters of precepts and beliefs, it is because they are seeking to *be* virtuous and to compose their own lives, rather than worrying that *others* might be vicious, leading discordant lives. Such teachers do the best that a teacher can do. In their own deliberations, they cast enough light that I may see something by it, if I happen to be looking.

Such teachers do not truly write books that might be called *How to Live*. Nor should there be such a book. There should be millions and millions of books, written down or not, called *How to Live (I Think)*. We would doubtless take some profit from passing our books around, from holding converse with each other, and quietly asking and answering in turn. But we would take nothing but discord and enmity from requiring of each other, as we regularly do, obedience to this or that version of *How to Live (I Think)*. The best that I can do for Petronilla—or for anybody else—is to make of my book something that will help her to write hers.

This is not that book. *How to Live (I Think)* is a book that can not be finished. But it is all too often a book that never begins. The first line is the hardest part, but whoever writes even that one line has passed at once into what Socrates called the examined life, the life that *is* worth living. So it is that we do well to listen to our wise parents, and borrow a line or two from them. Many a version of *How to Live (I Think)* can begin with the words of Epictetus, or Socrates, or of Tolstoy or Milton, or of some stranger on a train, or of some letter to the editor. The occasions of education that have been left for us by our parents are beyond counting, and so too are those we provide each other every day. That is the natural duty of any parent—to provide, again and again, that occasion for any child.

The largest and simplest definition of true education that I can imagine is this: It is all that is absent in the lives of those who aren't composing *How to Live (I Think)*.

ABOUT THE AUTHOR

Richard Mitchell is the *Underground Grammarian*, among other things. He is the author of *Less Than Words Can Say*, *The Graves of Academe*, and *The Leaning Tower of Babel*. He lives in New Jersey and likes it very much.